THIS IS THE VICTORY

THIS IS THE VICTORY

By
LESLIE D. WEATHERHEAD

"This is the victory that overcometh the
world, even our faith."

1 *John* v. 4, A.V.

LONDON
HODDER AND STOUGHTON LIMITED

DEDICATED

TO

ALFRED TORRIE

M.A., M.B., Ch.B., D.P.H., D.P.M.

A BELOVED PHYSICIAN

AND

MY DEAR FRIEND

First printed 1940

Printed and Bound in Great Britain for Hodder & Stoughton, Limited,
by Richard Clay and Company, Ltd., Bungay, Suffolk.

PREFACE

WHEN MY PUBLISHERS, FROM WHOM I HAVE received every possible courtesy, suggested that since " Thinking Aloud in Wartime " had helped many who are disturbed in mind and heart by war, I might attempt a sequel, I realised that the only way of meeting such a suggestion in these busy days would be to re-write and enlarge some of the messages which I have preached to my people at the City Temple during the last few months.

Thus this book took form, and thus the direct method of address is often retained and here and there ideas are repeated.

If anyone can say anything to anybody to help him face the appalling situation of the present time, perhaps no abject apology need be affixed to his effort. Anyway, this attempt to stiffen spiritual morale goes forth in the hope that it may help some who are feeling in soul as well as mind and body the intolerable strain of war.

I should like this Preface to provide some kind of background from which this book emerges. As I write these words in the autumn of the year of our Lord 1940, my house in London trembles with the vibration caused by the firing of guns, the explosion of bombs and the falling of houses. Last night my elder son and I went on duty for the local air-raid warden in order that he might get what chance there is of a night's sleep. The siren, warning the city of imminent air raids, wailed its melancholy message at dusk, and the " all clear " signal sounded just before six the next morning. All through the long, hideous night the din went on. In my neighbourhood five people were killed near one end of the road and three near the other. Night after night this is what is happening in London. Thousands are homeless. In one month seven thousand have been killed and ten thousand injured. Seven hundred of the killed were children under sixteen. Seven hundred of the injured were also children. Every evening multitudes take a three-

halfpenny ticket on the underground rail-
way, and, admitted to the platform, stay
there all night. If they queue up early
enough to get sufficient space, which some
do long before mid-day, they lie down. If
not, they stand up all night, and then,
hollow-eyed and weary, go to work the
next morning. Few military targets seem
to be hit, but hospitals, churches and homes
have been demolished. During the last
fortnight a quarter of a million pounds
worth of damage has been done to the
London property of one Christian denomination alone. Some areas look as if an
earthquake had taken place.

The work of the minister of religion can
easily be imagined. He must " carry on "
as far as possible, though daily his difficulties increase. People need God as never
before. Yet transport difficulties make both
the minister's visiting and a journey to
churches in Central London a matter of
hours. And people are so starved of sleep,
so tired of journeys, that who can blame
them if they stay at home? After dark it
is definitely foolish to be out unnecessarily.
The anti-aircraft barrage means that shrap-

nel often falls like hail. Every Londoner has two or three pieces on his mantelpiece, picked up near his home or in his gutters !

Many ministers are doing splendid service in air-raid shelters. Some of these shelters are beneath churches, and ministers have found that they have a resident congregation after the early afternoon !

All ministers find their visiting heart-breaking. I recall an afternoon in which I visited a paralysed boy, a family of ten with hardly a room left to them by the fires that raged all round them, two maiden ladies whose little business has almost come to an end through war, and a girl with both feet trapped by her falling house. Another girl from my church, bravely doing her duty as an A.R.P. warden, had her arm blown off by an explosion outside the warden's post.

My telephone bell rings. A doctor, a member of my church and a Harley Street specialist, asks whether I will go to such and such a hospital as soon as possible. A girl is lying there badly injured. Her sister was killed last night. Her mother has not yet been found, though men have been digging and searching ever since the house was demolished. Her father is dead also. I must try to comfort her. . . .

So day follows day in agony, sorrow and suffering. People are very brave. There is no doubt about that. And they believe Britain will win, though they wonder what meaning the word " win " will have. They keep a smile as near the surface as they can and they keep a stiff upper lip for the sake of those who have to live with them. But I cannot help feeling that underneath is a sense of futility and bewilderment not far from a kind of secret despair. " Where is it all going to end? " they ask.

And any glib talk about " cleaning up the world ", or " war to end war ", or " establishing a new order in Europe " is apt to make members of my generation either angry, cynical or silent, according to the temperament of the listener. We heard all that before, between 1914 and 1918. We lost our fathers and brothers and school chums then. Now our sons are wanted for the same bloody scheme.

In the obvious horrors around us we can't see the birth-pangs of a new era. It

is hard to understand just how the demo-
lition of my neighbour's house, bringing
sudden death to a father and mother and
three little girls, is going to make a brave
new world where the love of God will be
the operative factor and all man's discoveries and inventions turned into the
stream which serves his well-being and
happiness. Come to that, it isn't easy to
see how bombing Berlin, which many now
demand, will help much.

I went to the pictures one afternoon to
try to forget the horrors of war for a couple
of hours. But the news commentator used
" swine " and " Germans " as synonymous
terms, and told us there would be no peace
until we had " stamped out the whole race
of these vermin ". Yet many of " these
vermin " are friends and fellow-Christians,
and last summer one hundred and fifty
young people went from my church alone
on what we called a " Friendship Invasion "
of Germany to try to establish friendly
contact and make war impossible.

War is wrong. No one can identify
dropping bombs with the mind and will of
Christ. Yet I don't see how we could have

avoided this wrong without bringing a still greater wrong to generations ahead. It is no good being wise twenty-two years after the event and saying that we should have treated Germany differently in 1918. We sat back and watched the spirit of revenge incarnate itself in one who is determined to dominate all Europe, who has declared himself, and been declared by his minions to be, a greater than Christ,[1] who has waded to his place of despotic power through seas of innocent blood, who has enslaved nation after nation and people after people, who has no respect for the plighted word, no sense of honour or decency, who has en-

[1] Lest this should seem an exaggeration it may be recalled that in 1935 District Leader Becker said, " In later centuries, when one will have a true measure for things as they are to-day, it will be said, ' Christ was great, but Adolf Hitler was greater '." The Nazi Minister for Church Affairs said, " The question of the divinity of Christ is ridiculous and unessential. A new authority, Adolf Hitler, has arisen as to what Christ and Christianity really are."

Hitler himself said, " One is either a German or a Christian. You cannot be both. Do you really believe the masses will ever be Christian again? Nonsense! Never again! That tale is finished. No one will listen to it again." (I owe the quotations to a fine broadcast address by the Rev. R. F. V. Scott, Minister of St. Columba's, Pont Street, London.)

throned terror and treachery, violence and
ruthless persecution, spread more misery in
the world than any other human being
since time began, and who, if not resisted,
would end human liberty and justice, and,
with the instruments of the revolver, the
bomb and the lash, seek to bring us back
to those Dark Ages in which children's
minds are fed on pagan ideals and from
which all the finest movements of the
human spirit have sought to liberate man.

Hitler will never beat the spirit of the
British people, or blind their eyes, or bluff
their minds. They see the alternative to
resistance clearly before them. And though
the price they are asked to pay is hard and
heavy, they would rather part with the last
poor sticks of house and home, the last
drop of blood, and—hardest of all—they
would rather lose their dear ones under
their eyes and live—if life is left to them—
in a land impoverished for generations, than
have for their ruler in this dear, free, lovely
land the mad tyrant whose record is such
that death would be preferable to submission to him.

So I believe in Britain's cause. Victorious warfare may limit the scope of evil and check its influence even though it does little to eradicate that evil. The latter is spiritual, and can only be dealt with as the hearts of men are changed. But I am quite sure we shall never reach our war aims by calling one another "swine" and "vermin", by stirring up hate, by forgetting the thousands in "enemy" countries who are as unhappy as we are and long in their hearts for the rule of Christ.

We shall never be anything like fit as a nation to be used as God's instrument in the making of a world nearer to His heart's desire unless we can exorcise from our minds and hearts the spirit of bitterness, malice and hate, unless we can pray most of all for the victory of God's will, and regard our present suffering, not as the banked-up fires which, given their chance, shall devour Germany in flames of vengeance, but as the furnace in which our own spirits become purged and clean, ready to do the will of God with a single eye to His glory, and the true welfare of Europe and of the world.

So from this dear old London, now in an agony such as it has never known in all its

long history, goes forth this message : that
our true victory will depend on our faith in
God and His purposes in the world. " This
is the victory that overcometh the world,
even our faith."

LESLIE D. WEATHERHEAD.

The City Temple,
  London,
    November 1940.

NOTE

First of all I must thank my beloved
father-in-law, the Rev. Arthur Triggs, for
yet another kindness he has done me in
correcting the proofs of this book.

I wish to thank my friend Mr. Albert
Clare, Treasurer of the City Temple, Editor
of the *City Temple Tidings,* and author of
" The City Temple, 1640–1940," for so
kindly reading the proofs and making many
valuable suggestions.

My friend, Miss Alice M. Head, Editor of
Good Housekeeping, has most kindly allowed
me to use in this book material which, in

another form, appeared in that excellent magazine.

Miss Winifred Haddon has helped me considerably by taking down in shorthand addresses given from the pulpit which I have afterwards been able to work over. My secretary, Miss Margaret Fearn, has again devoted much attention to detail and has typed and re-typed the manuscript at a time when, in London, concentrated work has been specially difficult and often dangerous. I am deeply grateful for all this unstinted and valuable help.

L. D. W.

CONTENTS

PART III

FAITH'S FORWARD LOOK

THE ARGUMENT

PART I

PART I
"OUR FAITH"

CHAPTER ONE

FAITH IN PROGRESS SHATTERED

PART OF THE ANGRY BEWILDERMENT WHICH lies behind the exterior courage with which men and women are meeting the unprecedented calamity of these days is, in my view, due to a false, but deeply implanted belief that man had progressed beyond the possibilities of such barbarism as we have witnessed.

Before we can see what faith in God means I feel sure we must let faith in man go. To use an expressive, if ugly, modern phrase, we must " debunk " the idea of the inevitability of progress, an idea, it may be remembered, which is comparatively new in the thought of man. Plato believed in cycles some seventy-two thousand years in length. After the beginning of each new cycle man's estate was tolerably good. But it worsened, until the gods had to end it and create life anew. Marcus Aurelius thought little of the possibility of progress, for he wrote, " He who is forty years old, if he has any understanding at all, has, by virtue of the uniformity that prevails, seen all things which have been and all that will be."

It will be the theme of this chapter that no development is worth calling progress unless it be spiritual; the fruit of communion with God, a vision of His nature and purposes in the world, and the subsequent dedication of man's powers, inventions and discoveries to those purposes.

For years now the dominant ideas round about us have encouraged us to believe that humanity was progressing. The magic word " evolution " played its part especially as it was mediated through the poetry of Tennyson.[1] The idea, true in the biological realm, was eagerly carried over even by Darwin himself [2] into realms in which it

[1] cf. *Locksley Hall*.
[2] " As natural selection works solely by and for the good of each being, all corporeal and mental environments will tend to progress towards perfection." Darwin, " Origin of Species."

certainly did not apply. The thought took root in men's minds that physically, mentally and spiritually mankind was in an elevator, and, as they say at the stores, " going up ". Huxley, one of the most eminent interpreters of evolution, gives no support to this misinterpretation of the doctrine. " Man is a brute ", he wrote, " even the best of modern civilisations appears to me to exhibit a condition of mankind which neither embodies any worthy ideal nor even possesses the merit of stability. . . . The theory of evolution encourages no millennial anticipations." But Herbert Spencer, the philosopher of Evolution, wrote, "Progress is not an accident nor a thing within human control, but a beneficent necessity. This advancement is due to the working of a universal law . . . in virtue of that law it must combine until the state we call perfection is reached. . . . What we call evil and immorality must disappear. It is certain that man must become perfect." Sadly enough now, we see no reason for the use of the word " must ". Modern man may respond to his friend by means of the telephone instead of the letter which served in earlier days, but the content of the response is not thus altered, and no speeding up of methods of man's response to man leads him to that response to God which is the only test of true progress.

The Coué doctrines, widely promulgated, had an effect far beyond their legitimate sphere. A miner's lungs, we are told, are black with coal-dust, though he is unaware of it. The minds of men and women are full of the ideas floating about in the mental atmosphere they breathe, although they give to those ideas no conscious approval or consent.

So when folk were being told of the progress they could make mentally and physically by throwing open the bedroom window and saying, " Every day in every way I am getting better and better ", the thought of progress attainable by just believing that it was happening took hold of many minds in ways Coué never dreamed of in his most enthusiastic moments.

How differently psychologists talk today ! What abysmal depths of wickedness are opened up before our eyes by Freud's

picture of the unconscious part of our minds !
And listen to Jung, for he sounds a note
which we must heed or perish. " Freud
has unfortunately overlooked the fact that
man has never yet been able single-handed
to hold his own against the powers of darkness—that is, of the unconscious. Man
has always stood in need of the spiritual
help which each individual's own religion
held out to him. . . . Man is never helped
in his suffering by what he thinks for himself, but only by revelations of a wisdom
greater than his own. It is this which lifts
him out of his distress." [1]

Another factor for which we may be
thankful, but which again produces an
illusion, is the attention to social reform.
It is good that the slums should go, that
drunkenness and immorality should be
fought and made difficult. But when you
have done all these outward and good things
you have not necessarily done much towards
progress, unless you have also done something to change men's hearts. If this were
not true, then, to establish the Kingdom of

[1] Jung, " Modern Man in Search of a Soul," pp.
277-8 (Kegan Paul).

Heaven, as most people think of it, all you would have to do would be to exclude sickness and disease, give every man a job, a house and a nice garden, a few lectures on art and sanitation and culture, and acclaim your " progressive " policy. But the facts go to show that the people who most obstruct progress are those who already have a nice house with hot and cold in all the bedrooms—have, in fact, all that money can acquire—but have also a greed and selfishness which postpone for generation after generation the sharing of God's good gifts, and which know nothing of the changed heart which makes a man look up into the face of God and call Him " Father ", and into the faces of all nations and peoples and call them all " brothers ".

There is nothing in my heart but sincere praise for the social-welfare clinics, the slum-abolition societies, the temperance and purity committees and the young ladies with diplomas who are so intent to build Jerusalem in England's green and pleasant land. All that is good although every psychologist knows how often such reforming zeal is unconsciously motivated by some inner problem of frustration or personal dissatisfaction in the deep mind of the social worker. It is philanthropy, if it is not religion. Whether it is progress depends on the state of the heart of the man for whom all this is being done and the state of the heart of the doer. I have camped on the site of Babylon. I have seen the signs of culture in Egypt. I have walked round the ruins of Pompeii where you are shown the hot baths offered to the poor and many other signs of " civilisation " and " progress ". But the Babylonian, Egyptian and Roman civilisations went out into the darkness because Babylon, Egypt and Rome were civilisations which God could no longer use. To ameliorate outward conditions is a work which must be done. It must win God's approval. Whether it marks progress depends on what the man does with the life that is made happier for him. To invent the aeroplane is an amoral act. It is without moral significance. Everything depends on the use made of the aeroplane. It might succour the starving in a desert place, or bring medical aid to the isolated, and become a blessing. It might be used to bomb women and children and be accursed. To provide a man with a house or a job or an income is amoral. Everything depends on what he does with his amenities.

So we come to the scientific discoveries which, more than any other factors, have created an illusion of progress. We will spend a moment looking at these, but I will beg the question at once by asking the reader to put side by side in his mind the picture of the man of a million years ago, wrapped in skins, snatching up his club and making for his cave because his enemy is in sight, with the picture of a friend of mine snatching his gas-mask and making for a cave dug in his garden because enemy 'planes are in sight. My friend may have been educated at Oxford, may have in his cave a wireless set, modern sanitation, electric light and heat, but while one admits *development*, I wonder if the word " progress " is the right word to use. Last night in London life was terrifying, harassing and sleepless, physical safety and peace of mind were harder to find, danger was more wide-spread, the kind of death that threatened more horrible, the scale of disaster more appalling than was the case before the Romans invaded Britain.

I am far from depreciating the immense development man has made in his conquest of the forces of Nature and his harnessing of them to his plans. Let us try to realise just how immense as well as recent that development has been.

I am going to imagine that the entire " progress " of the race is represented by a period of fifty years. This is for many a mentally compassable period, and carries more meaning than descriptive writing in terms of tens of millions of years.

Until forty-nine of the fifty years were over man would not have begun to be " civilised " at all. Having emerged to something worth calling human, he would still be hunting with primitive weapons. He would have no settled abode. Yet mark the sudden and swift change. Half-way through the fiftieth year he invents writing. Only in the last two months of the fiftieth year would he know the blessings of Christianity. His printing-press would be only a fortnight old. And only in the last week did he travel by road. An hour or two ago he learned to fly.[1]

We all have ways of bringing home to our minds the wonders of Science. We all have our choice of scientific gadgets which it thrills us to think about. To me one of the most amazing is the instrument at broadcasting stations which records roughly how many sets are tuned in, or, as one engineer put it to me, what load the ether is carrying.

I read recently that a robot was exhibited at the Chicago World Fair a year ago. You pressed a button in the middle of its chest and it opened its mouth and gave orders by wireless to another robot in a neighbouring field, which proceeded to plough the field as efficiently as any man could plough it. Visitors to the exhibition were told that the vast prairies could be standardised and ploughed by robots all set in motion by a single man pressing a button in Washington.

The conquest of distance thrills the

[1] I have borrowed this method of presenting facts from James Harvey Robinson, " The Mind in the Making " (Harper).

imagination as illustrative of the immense " progress " made and its suddenness. Until the locomotive was developed by Stephenson in 1814, from an earlier invention, no man could travel over the earth's surface faster than a horse could run. John Wesley could travel no faster than Pharaoh. Yet comparatively within the last few minutes of man's strange history a train has reached the speed of 126 m.p.h., a car 370, and a 'plane 469. The *Queen Mary* took me to America at between 30 and 40 m.p.h., and I suppose a submarine could have raced her at the bottom of the sea.[1] Distance is almost annihilated. Compare the sending of a message from a ship by

[1] An American train is reported to have reached 143 m.p.h., but was electrically driven and a propeller was used, so that it can scarcely be called a locomotive.

John Cobb's racing automobile reached 370·8 m.p.h. on Salt Lake Flats, Utah, in 1939. Malcolm Campbell reached 142·9 m.p.h. on water.

It is hard to say what speed a modern 'plane can now do. 469 m.p.h. was reached by a fighter plane last year (1939), but in a power dive a Hawker Hurricane has reached 600 m.p.h.

The *Normandie* (French) beat the *Queen Mary* by 0·5 knots, reaching 28·5 knots, or 33 m.p.h.

semaphore to the coast, and thus by horse-
men to the capital, with wireless news that
tells us over our dinner-tables what happened in Tokio an hour ago.

One sometimes imagines a watcher of
this planet rejoicing in man's advances,
how he has wrested Nature's powers to
serve him, annihilated distance and created
wealth. One imagines such a watcher
smiling to think how happy life could be
for all very soon. God has given the good
things of earth in such profusion and gifted
man with such energy of discovery and
invention. All the work of the world could
be done in a four-day week. Indeed, Lord
Leverhulme once said, " With the means
that science has already placed at our disposal we might provide for all the wants
of each of us in food, shelter and clothing
by one hour's work per week for each
of us from school age to dotage." And
the Continental Committee of Technocratic
Enquiry of the United States, after a three-
year investigation of the productive capacity
of American industry, reported that if
American industry worked to capacity, an
income of £700 a year could be guaranteed

to every American family of four persons.[1]
It is scientifically possible to banish poverty
from the earth. There need be no hunger,
or unemployment, or slums, or sweating, or
fear. Illness and disease could probably
be mastered in a short period if all the
resources of the human family were concentrated on the effort. When Professor
Sydney Smith presented candidates for their
medical degrees at Edinburgh last summer
(1940), he told them that " more advance
had been made in the past fifty years than
in the whole of human history " and he
expected that speed to be maintained.
Ten years, he said, had been added to the
mean expectation of life, the death rate had
fallen and disease was gradually being
exterminated.

There could be time for music and art, for
games and fun, for revelling in Nature's
glories, for creative work and for the
worship of the Giver of all.

But in imagination one sees the smile fade
on the face of the watcher. Man has
wrested from Nature her secrets. He can

[1] I owe these quotations to D. R. Davies, " On to
Orthodoxy," p. 38 (Hodder & Stoughton).

turn her vast energies to his purposes. His fertile, unresting mind has put discovery after discovery, invention after invention at human disposal. But we can take little pride in the annihilation of distance and the ingenuity of man when we think of the errand of the bombing aeroplane. A good man on horseback is a better symbol of progress than a bad man in a 'plane.

Man has laboured to increase the wealth of the world, and has done so. An artisan earning fifty shillings a week possesses things which would have made Solomon's mouth water and the Queen of Sheba faint. But the excessive production with which Nature has rewarded man's effort has been dealt with in so selfish a spirit that a few are very rich, while millions are very poor. It is a platitude, but a terrible comment on " progress ", that while thousands are in real need, corn is burned in Canada, coffee in Brazil, rubber in Africa, fish thrown back into the sea and apples left rotting on the ground. Worst of all, as I write these words the greatest nations of the world are all bending their strength of heart and brain and hand to find out how they can most effectively and speedily kill their fellows. No wonder the watcher ceases to smile ! The means of life have been so misused that the meaning of life is for most people totally obscured.

Obviously, so far from calling the present trend of things progress, we can only view it with dismay. When spiritual responsibility does not keep pace with material discovery and invention, true progress ceases. It may not appear to cease. There may be a certain impressiveness as the discoveries follow one another. But the alleged progress might be compared with erecting a building, storey upon storey, to a height more and more impressive, without any attention to the foundations. Unless the foundations are deep enough and strong enough, or else strengthened as the building goes up, then the increased height means an increased menace to those whom " science " set out to serve, and when the building crashes it is pardonable to wish that one were back in the era of mud huts.

" John Mason would, in my opinion," said George Arliss, " have been the greatest actor in America *if his private character had been as well balanced as his public performances.*"

A similar comment could be made on modern life.

As Dr. Fosdick finely says,[1] " They are having trouble with the housing problem in Tokyo, and the reason is simple. Tokyo is built on earthquake ground, and it is insecure. You cannot put great houses on unstable foundations. . . . But in New York City one sees the skyscrapers reaching up their sixty storeys into the air. The explanation is not difficult: Manhattan Island is solid rock. If you are going to build great structures you must have great foundations. And civilisation is a vast and complicated structure. We cannot build it on physical force. That is too shaky. We must build it on spiritual foundations."

It is hard to learn the truth about Russia, but if one is not utterly mistaken we have the spectacle of a country which a score of years ago set out to make itself a progressive State. The revolution cost the lives of tens of thousands of innocent people, but no returning traveller talks as if Russia revealed the conditions of the Kingdom of Heaven on earth. One would not be surprised if it

[1] " Christianity and Progress," p. 73 (Nisbet).

soon became obvious that Russia is the greatest menace to Europe's true well-being. Its leader exhibits a cold, treacherous tyranny compared with which the sway of the Tsars was as benign as that of Father Christmas.

The fact we forget, and which people hate hearing mentioned, is the fact of sin. Man is innately selfish. He is a glorious creature, and can be made to behave like a son of God, but not by telling him he is an escalator called " Evolution ", not by changing his environment, giving him new programmes or ideologies or " isms ", not by telling him he is getting better and better every day—not even by frightening him. No modernism, no culture, no Act of Parliament, no education, no scientific discovery, no outward influence will override the fact of original sin or lessen the strength of its pull. It may restrain its pull and shame its expression, but it is still there. Man is better in many ways than he was a thousand years ago, but definitely worse in other ways. There is not enough in it to make us talk about progress.[1]

[1] If this seems an exaggerated statement I would

In 1770 Sebastien Mercier described what civilisation would be like in 2440 A.D. Every one would have work, labour would be minimised and so on. But J. B. Bury in his book, " The Idea of Progress," (1920), commenting on Mercier's prophecies, says wisely that the two things Mercier does not allow for are the strength of human passions and interests, and a deficient appreciation of the meaning of liberty.

We must settle down to the fact that unaided man is incapable of building a just world, let alone a perfect world. Even Mr. Joad in " Why War? " says, " Evil will never be eradicated from human nature." " Never " is a word which wise men never use ! But it certainly is improbable that evil will be eradicated by culture and civilisation and the things external to the spirit of man. Great civilisations, in their way as great as ours, have simply disappeared from the face of the earth. Is there really any reason why ours should not follow them ? It gives one a very queer

urge the reader to study D. R. Davies's book, " On to Orthodoxy" (H. & S.), a vigorous exposure of the illusion of progress and the pretensions of humanism.

feeling in regard to one's own civilisation to talk, as I have done, among the ruins of Babylon, to an Arab who was quite illiterate. It seems almost incredible that a great civilisation like that centred in modern London can pass away. But it may. The melancholy history of earlier civilisations points to the possibility of future illiterate peasants living in mud huts over the present site of Piccadilly Circus and Leicester Square.

This is not a wholly depressing thought to the Christian. For man's perfection and history's *dénouement* may be in the world which follows this. We are bidden pray for the coming of Christ's Kingdom on earth; and as men's hearts are changed by the spirit of Christ, *real* progress can be achieved, for men will learn to love and find the only dynamic there is for love : the character of God and communion with Him. But did not Christ Himself tell us to expect wars and rumours of wars up to the very end of the world? And war is not merely a temporary lapse in an inevitable progress. It shows man morally back on the old grim level of hate. His culture only makes his wars more ghastly and extensive.

To put the realisation of Christ's dream of the coming of the Kingdom in the next world will seem to some like the old cry of " pie in the sky when you die ", but to look round the world makes one more than suspicious that unless there is new and powerful co-operation with a Power greater than man's, there is little chance of pie anywhere else, and surely we are not for ever to remain hungry. The man who to-day is putting his money on this world seems a bit of a gambler.

Nor would such a conception spell the failure of the Church on earth. A school exists to train men and women for the life which follows schooldays rather than merely to adorn the school. I remember going back to my old school after I had left it. It didn't seem to have improved much. The blackboards and the wall-maps were better, the desks were superior, and incandescent burners had given place to electric light. But not by such things does a school make *progress*. Two boys were waiting to be caned outside the headmaster's study, just where I once waited ! A class deserted by a teacher became at once an unruly, excited mob bent on mischief, just as I had helped it to be when I was at school. Smith minor was evidently still incapable of keeping ink off his collar and jam off his ears—and so on. Why hadn't the school progressed?— Because human nature is the same, and unredeemed human nature keeps coming in at the junior end of the school ! Perfection won't come *in* the school, though there is splendid development. Progress is rather seen in the higher forms as against the lower, not in the school at one period of history as against another.

The world is a school. There is development, but progress is to be judged by the level reached by those in the higher forms, not by one period of the world-school life compared with another. For only the outward paraphernalia—like blackboards in the school of our youth—are improved. " If Ruth came back ", I once heard Dr. Fosdick say, " we should put her sickle in a museum, for we have vast machines which storm across the prairie and do the work of a thousand men; but Ruth in her loyalty to her mother-in-law would put us to shame. We have improved on Ruth's sickle, but have we improved on Ruth? "

But the illustration of the school breaks down, and in this there is hope. For here on earth sometimes the supernatural life of the beyond breaks in on a lowly human heart, and a man or woman becomes a partaker in the redeemed life. *Then* you have progress on earth, because you have response to God. And if sufficient men and women are thus changed from above, they may see the Kingdom of Heaven come on earth. " The world will continue to improve," said Southey in 1829, " even as it has hitherto been continually improving; and the progress of knowledge and the diffusion of Christianity will bring about at last, *when men become Christian in reality as well as in name,* something like that Utopian state of which philosophers have loved to dream." [1] Whether that is God's purpose or not I do not know.

The supreme fact of life, and the only one that gives us any hope of progress at all, is

[1] Quoted from J. B. Bury, " The Idea of Progress," p. 325.

that man can turn to God, and open his heart to God and be used by God. Only thus does man learn to love, to be kind and unselfish, and all so-called progress which leaves out love is development, but in no sense progress. Chromium plate and television and electric gadgets never yet made one man love another man. It is rather development towards disaster, because man, still unchanged, still selfish, will use his developed powers to bring even greater evil on mankind as a result of his selfishness and sin.

It is beyond the power of human effort to create the perfect society, and to spend one's life labouring for social changes which only bring new masters who become tyrants as soon as they get power, and new injustices and new cruelties, is just wasting time. We change the stage-scenery, but the plot is the same. Characters come and go, but, save for the twice-born, who are usually crucified, they play the same part and say the same things.

The one hope of the world is that God has a plot, in which man can play a part, a plan for His school-world which could make life happier here, but, better still,

points to a further plan on another stage.
And wonderful though it is to say so—so
wonderful as to be thought incredible—God
has entered human life, come on to our stage,
worn our make-up, to show what life could
be. And He offers to enter our lives. In
not many cases has He done so, though
with some He has made a beginning, which,
though small and disappointing, leads us to
hope. But when we see a life wholly surrendered to God we know that real progress
is possible in this old world, and if the
wholly surrendered cannot change life in
this setting, they are a promise of a further
life in which all men's deepest longings shall
be realised and all God's dreams come true.

Some of what has been written may seem
pessimistic. Frankly, if God be left out and
the supernatural be excluded, I see no hope
for the world. There is nothing in history
which proves an inevitable progress, no
ground for supposing that man—without
God—will ever improve. He will talk
through telephones, no doubt, travel in air-
liners, be entertained by television, fight
diseases, tackle his housing and unemployment and industrial problems, but will he—

without God—become unselfish? Will he ever understand the meaning, let alone the practice, of love?

Our philosophy of life has broken down. We could not believe that in these " progressive " days mankind would slip back to the bestial. Even Gibbon wrote, " we cannot determine to what height the human species may aspire in their advances towards perfection; but it may safely be presumed that no people, unless the face of nature is changed, will relapse into their original barbarism." [1] So if faith is to be revived—faith in the victory of God—we need a new philosophy of life. And though I may tell myself that if I believe in God I may still believe in progress, one wonders whether the God one believes in is the real God, or a small-sized, conventional idol whom I have been calling God by mistake. I know that only by faith can I find victory over that paralysing, depressing thought that final darkness is descending on the world. But I need faith in the real God if ever I am to say with conviction, " This is the victory that overcometh, even our faith."

[1] "Decline and Fall of the Roman Empire," Chap. 38.

CHAPTER TWO

FAITH IN LIFE'S WORTH-WHILENESS WANTED

UNFORTUNATELY THE WORD " FAITH " IS SO surrounded in most minds with theological implications—amongst them the schoolboy's supposition that faith is believing what you know to be untrue—that it is less confusing to use the phrase, " a philosophy of life ". We need, then, a set of ideas which the mind tenaciously holds, ideas big enough and strong enough to help us face the demands which life is making upon us.

In the last war men used to say, " If my name is on a bullet it will get me ; if it's not, I shall be O.K. ! " I've heard an air-raid warden say the same kind of thing about a German bomb and proceed to take unnecessary risks. Presumably his philosophy of life was a kind of fatalism that what was ordained would come to pass whatever he did about it. I suppose he never stopped to ask what sort of God it was—for surely God is implied—who wrote the names of a father and mother and three little girls on a bomb that fell near my house and killed them all. Others hold what I regard as strange views about ancient prophecy, and I have met those who even seem elated at some new calamity because it fits in to the scheme worked out from queer interpretations of isolated verses in Daniel, Ezekiel or Revelation.

Sound or unsound, men feel the need of some kind of philosophy of life. What the mind cannot tolerate is meaninglessness. And certainly if we once allowed ourselves to sink in that morass, if it were our faith or philosophy that nothing mattered, that nothing had meaning or significance, that nothing had any worthwhileness or value, that no plan or purpose was being worked out, then there would be no victory for us— our morale would be broken, our spiritual defeat certain. And, of course, if that happened to everyone, the nation itself would be morally defeated and quite unfitted to be an instrument in the hands of God for the making of a new world. In a

D

sentence, life must make sense and be worthwhile. The existence of some cults is due to man's quest for meaningfulness. The philosophy of life previously held broke down at some point where meaningfulness was most needed, so the seeker turned to a new philosophy which, at the relevant point, seemed to make sense. Spiritualism has thus been adopted by many who couldn't make sense of death. Christian Science has been adopted by many who couldn't make sense of disease. The strength of both these cults is, in a way, a valid criticism of orthodox Christianity. Without attempting to say whose fault it may have been, at those points orthodoxy failed to provide meaningfulness. The philosophy of life broke down. Faith was not adequate. People want to live victoriously, and faith is the only way of getting the victory over circumstance. We must have an adequate faith.

Now we have reached a time of great testing for religion. In the Christian philosophy of life, truly understood, I believe there is an adequate faith for this or any situation. Christianity has an answer to—not necessarily an explanation of—every situation. Or, if I may put it thus, if Christianity does not know the answer, it believes that there *is* an answer, which is all that matters. Whether men will give the Church a chance, and whether, given the chance, the Church can rise to the needs of men's minds, remains to be seen.

It is certain that the little God and little faith which proved adequate for the little lives which little men mostly lived in the prolonged and uneasy truce between 1918 and 1939 will certainly not do for today. Our philosophy of life must be stretched to meet the terrific needs of today. The process described in a poem of Samuel Foss is of immense importance.

> A boy was born 'mid little things,
> Between a little world and sky,
> And dreamed not of the cosmic rings
> 'Round which the circling planets fly.
>
> He lived in little works and thoughts,
> Where little ventures grow and plod,
> And paced and ploughed his little plots,
> And prayed unto his little God.
>
> But, as the mighty system grew,
> His faith grew faint with many scars;
> The cosmos widened in his view,
> But God was lost among his stars.

Another boy in lowly days,
As he, to little things was born,
But gathered lore in woodland ways,
And from the glory of the morn.

As wider skies broke on his view,
God greatened in his growing mind;
Each year he dreamed his God anew,
And left his older God behind.

He saw the boundless scheme dilate,
In star and blossom, sky and clod;
And, as the universe grew great,
He dreamed for it a greater God.

Think of life for, say, a suburban bank-clerk in the years mentioned above. The circle of life was small. It revolved mainly, shall we say, in Golder's Green? The branch of the bank at which he worked was in Golder's Green. His nice little house, with the privet hedge in front and the sunflowers and Michaelmas daisies at the back, was in Golder's Green. On Sundays he worshipped at Golder's Green. On Saturday afternoons he played bowls at Golder's Green Bowling Club, and on Saturday evenings he took his wife to the pictures at Golder's Green Cinema.

The circle of her life was no bigger. She shopped at Golder's Green, changed her

books at Smith's library at Golder's Green.
She went one afternoon a week to the
Sewing Meeting at the Church in Golder's
Green. The spirit of daring adventure
pressed her some fine Saturdays to take a
morning coffee in the midst of her shopping
at Golder's Green !

Occasionally, and if visitors came to see
London, our friends took them up to Town
to see St. Paul's and " do " a theatre. But
St. Paul's having been seen and the theatre
safely " done " and the visitors seen off at
Golder's Green Tube Station, they settled
down again at Golder's Green. There were
holidays, of course, that sometimes became
wildly adventurous and took them near the
more comfortable mountains of Switzerland,
gave them a night in Paris, with a most
deliciously wicked feeling, making them
wonder what the vicar of Golder's Green
would think of them if he knew. There
were films which opened the world a bit to
them, but it was a garish, wild world, in
which they were not asked to take more
than a passing interest, being allowed to
view it from the safety of Golder's Green.
When they came out of " the pictures ", they

were still in Golder's Green. There were books and plays on the wireless . . . but they could rise and yawn and lock up the little house in Golder's Green, say a conventional prayer to the God who looked after Golder's Green, and then go to bed. Golder's Green would be there in the morning.

Then came this war. One had hardly heard of Sudeten Germans. One wasn't quite sure whether Warsaw was in Poland or in Russia. One would have been hard put to it to place Helsinki on a map. Very soon the circle of nearly every one's thought —life, even in Golder's Green, enclosed them all. One dark day Belgium and Holland were invaded. Thank God there was still the Maginot Line to hold back hell from Golder's Green. . . . France laid down her arms . . . Dunkirk . . . and then, in a month or two, German bombs were dropping in Golder's Green. Life is now a terrifying business.

The God who was big enough for the world the bank-clerk and his wife lived in doesn't seem relevant now. It was all right to think of Him occasionally, on bright Sunday mornings in the church at the

corner where the bus stops, when the choir
sang a tuneful anthem, and a pretty good
congregation sang heartily a lusty tune, and
the Vicar told you exactly what the Psalmist
meant when he expressed his intention of
lifting his eyes to the hills. . . . But now !
A brother is missing at Dunkirk. A brother-
in-law's business has come to a sudden end.
A sister is in the A.T.S., and our bank-clerk
has listened to terrifying lectures on the
structure of a bomb eight feet high and how
to deal with the effects of mustard gas. A
house at the end of his road has been demolished and his own dining-room windows
have been blown in.

Perhaps it is better not to think of God
at all. . . . Perhaps those are right who
threw God over at once. For how can there
be a God who allows this ? And why doesn't
God intervene ? Our friend doesn't stop to
ask why it didn't worry him that China and
Spain and Finland and Norway, Belgium
and Holland and France had faced all
this, and he never worried then about
what God was doing; that he had never
asked just at what point God should intervene in man's free will, now, or twenty

years ago, or in 1913 or earlier, perhaps
when man was created. . . . Nor was our
friend a bit clear what he thought God ought
to do about it, except finish off Hitler and
divert a bomb from his home and his dear
ones. He had always been a decent-living
chap. . . .

I am trying to show by these uncompleted
sentences how, for thousands, a philosophy
of life that has proved sufficient because no
serious test has ever been applied to it and
no attempt has been made to think it
through, has cracked and broken and
people are faced with a dilemma. They
must put their thoughts of God into cold-
storage until after the war, when, they hope,
their little God will be big enough for their
little lives. Or they must enlarge their
views of God to take in life as life now is for
thousands, a life which may end—in London,
at least, at the time I am writing—any
evening between dusk and dawn, and in any
case a life from which, at a stroke, everything may be taken which is usually thought
to make existence tolerable.

It is in the hope of helping some to get
an adequate philosophy of life that these

pages are being penned. If only one could show people Christ; if only one could show folk what real Christianity is, one could meet their need. For Christ Himself was driven from all security save God and His own relationship with God. Christ was stripped of everything save the certainty that He was the Son of God, that life has meaning, beauty and purpose, that no power of evil can touch the spirit or defeat God at last, that truth, beauty and goodness have eternal worth-whileness, and that the soul that lives in God is for ever safe and on its way to blessedness.

If men are in quest for God it should not trouble us unduly, even if their motive is that they are frightened and unhappy. If war itself acts as a high explosive to blow us out of the shelters we made for ourselves and in which we sought to hide from Him in a complacent, conventional evasiveness made up of lies and half-truths and scarcely-believed platitudes, it will prove another example of the way in which God uses man's evil to achieve His own good purposes. There are worse conditions of mind than being frightened, unhappy, or even in despair.

After all, belief is, in a sense, motived by the fear of unbelief, which is often the fear of meaninglessness. I do not mean that that which is believed has no other support than man's wishful thinking. In Christianity the great doctrines have objective bases and great historic facts behind them. I mean that the mental activity of believing is pressed upon men by the terror of the opposite. Men believe most readily when the opposite of believing would be to plunge them into the morass of meaninglessness.

Thus I believe in God not only because the evidence leads me so to believe, but because the alternative is chaos. Life makes no sense. The richest experiences of life would have to be dismissed as subjective illusions. Thus the mental act of believing is pressed upon me. I believe in immortality not only because the evidence of survival is to me convincing, but because life is meaningless if death ends it. I believe in the atonement not only because Jesus died upon the Cross a death which was relevant to human sin, but because the alternative is incredible. It lands me in meaninglessness to suppose that God did nothing to deal with human sin, especially now, when I can see more clearly than ever that certainly man can do nothing about his sins.

No wonder that men who have not put God away for the duration of the war are eagerly asking questions about Him.   They are hurled towards believing by the fact that not to believe that God is adequate to human life, whatever happens, is to be lost in meaninglessness.   The world becomes a badly run lunatic asylum without even the safeguards of the latter against self-destruction.

It would be worth fighting for this alone if not to fight meant that all Europe would become the kind of mad-house that Germany now is, where pagan ideals have been re-established and taught to children, truth distorted to fit ready-made theories, terror and tyranny brought back from the dark ages as means of imposing the tyrant's will, and man regarded merely as a means to an end, and where no philosophy of life that meets all situations is even allowed.

We are fighting, then, for our philosophy of life, which we call Christian, and it would be well if we understood it a little better. It is a fight for civilisation—which I should define as that condition in society in which man is held to be precious not as a means to an end, but as an end in himself,[1] and in which truth is regarded as an ultimate value, to be pursued for its own sake and followed wherever it may lead. If the definition be allowed, Germany is decivilising herself. She does not regard man as an end. The State is the end. Man is only a means. She does not regard truth as an ultimate value. German professors must not teach what is taught in every other university in the world, lest it conflicts with Hitler's theories.

But our fight is for a philosophy of life in which Christianity has a chance. The difference between winning and losing will be the difference between a country which at any rate *might* become Christian and in which Christian ideals are at any rate respected, a country which would be a ground

[1] Much in industry is seen to be barbarous as against civilised, since man is in many instances still regarded as a cog in a machine. I recognise that many ancient civilisations were not civilised in this sense.

in which the Christian values could take
root and flourish, and, on the other hand,
a country in which they are definitely
denied. Victory would make a Christian
peace possible. Defeat would make it impossible. Whether war will actually spread
Christianity may be doubted. Usually the
fruits which follow any war, waged with
never such good intentions, are mainly evil.
But war can, and we hope will, limit the
area of evil, strike at the power of that evil
to enslave more and yet more lives, and
prepare the way for a Christian solution of
our problems.

One is not surprised to hear that the
Germans are fighting with a zeal which is
almost religious. Where the Nazi mental
infiltration is complete, the State is God
and the Führer divine. Should such a
State be beaten, God for German Nazis is
dead.

The Christian philosophy of life, however,
stands whether we win or lose. I know no
other philosophy that guarantees spiritual
victory, whether that victory be interpreted
in the success or the defeat of arms. Defeat
is unlikely, many think impossible, but we

may take a leaf out of the book of the
Israelites in Old Testament days. When
they were defeated they only saw, in the
defeat, God using their enemies as a means
of disciplining them, a rod in the divine
hands. His purposes went on undefeated,
and *spiritual* victory was assured and
assured through *them*. If, on the other
hand, they won, it was always by the
Divine favour, never their mere numbers,
or prowess, or leadership, and it was always
that *God's* plans and purposes might be
furthered.

Whether we lose or win, God will win.
If we lose, we must ask God to show us
how defeat can be best used for His victory.
If we win—as I think we shall—we must
pray to be made worthy of victory and we
must use victory consciously for His ends.

During some very dark days a minister
rang me up and said he just didn't know
what to say to people in such a dark hour.
It was only a temporary depression. He
soon recovered, and can minister to his
people better than I. But, trying to help
him, I wrote down some things which are
part of my faith, and some of which I was

privileged to broadcast in the five-minute talks called, " Lift Up Your Hearts ". To me they partly express a philosophy of life which makes it worthwhile. They may serve to sum up this chapter.

1. God will win whether we win or lose. So in God, if we remain loyal to Him, the victory will be ours, even if it looks like defeat and is called defeat and feels like defeat. The Cross felt like defeat to Jesus, and looked like defeat to the disciples, and was called defeat by the world. Yet it was God's greatest victory. Let us, then, *prepare for victory*, be worthy of it and know how to apply it for God's purposes. If God could turn even the Cross to victory there is no disaster He could not turn to spiritual gain if we believed in Him.

2. It is grand, in an hour like this, to realise that Christ MUST reign, that nothing can drive Him from the hearts of those who love Him, or make His cause to perish in the earth.

3. The Church has gone through all this kind of thing before. This is not

her darkest hour. And as we recall the Church's dark days, we recall most readily and vividly not the persecutions, not " how awful that man Nero was!", but how gloriously shone the faith of the saints and martyrs. Let us be ready to follow in their train.

4. We are appalled at the loss of life. Yet there is no such thing as *loss* of life, only life transferred to another phase beyond the reach of bombs and beast-liness.

5. It is not what happens to us that matters most : it is our reaction to what happens to us that matters. Nothing would be allowed to happen if it had power of itself—apart from our reaction— to separate us from God. So the measure of calamity is the measure of the extent to which God trusts us to use it for good. If it could not possibly bring blessedness, if no possible reaction could make it work out for good, it would not be allowed, by a good God, to befall us.

6. Some of our children—to put things at their very worst—somewhere, will escape the power of the enemy. In

some hearts somewhere the ideals we cherish will live on. One day, sooner or later, if we have fallen in the fight, they will arise and unfurl the flag, and the winds of freedom that blow around God's throne will waft it so that others see it and rise to plant it again amongst men.

7. Every bit of sorrow and calamity we are called upon to endure can be used to buy back from the universe something greater in measure of blessedness than the measure of woe.

8. The measure of calamity must be less than the measure of God's ability to deal with it adequately, and the measure of our faith that He can do so must rise accordingly.

9. Calamity always tests faith. Severe calamity severely tests faith. But is not the severity some measure of the quality of the faith that is being tested? God would not test the quality of wood with fire. The fierceness of the fire points to gold.

These truths—platitudes to some, perhaps—are part of a Christian philosophy of

E

life, part of a faith which one seeks to strengthen and fortify at its source. And inner victory is there in that faith. But its centre must not be in a mere optimism that " all will turn out all right anyway, because God will see that it does so ". We must turn to consider the necessity of centering our faith in the real God, the God and Father of our Lord Jesus Christ. Then with a sense of reality we can say, " This is the victory that overcometh, even our faith ".

CHAPTER THREE

FAITH IN GOD ESSENTIAL

WHEN THE WORST DARKNESS THE WORLD has ever known was falling, when the stage was set for its most appalling tragedy, Jesus said, " Let not your heart be troubled, ye believe in God." Many of us have never been, and will never again be, called upon to face a darker time than that through which we are now passing. Can we too find fortitude from all that is implied in these words?

There is no wisdom in refusing to face reality. We are in search of an adequate philosophy of life with which to meet the present emergency. Such a philosophy of life will not be based on a facile optimism which has not taken dark facts into its reckoning. Neither will it be based on a gloomy pessimism which leaves on one side as irrelevant the glorious truths about God which Jesus revealed—truths which make

67

clear the complete adequacy of God for any situation that may arise.

The words of Christ to His sorrowing men come to us today as freshly and as truly as on the night they were spoken. If they were adequate for the need of the disciples, they can prove adequate for us. " Let not your heart be troubled, ye believe in God."

But do we? In many of our undertakings, nationally and individually, we have left God out altogether. There is perhaps little value now in recalling our indifference to the claims of God, the neglect of public worship, the slackness with which we have regarded His holy day, the careless treatment of the religious education of children, the hatred of all self-discipline and the selfish love of ease and pleasure and entertainment, the apathy of our social conscience, the weak longing for the things which peace brings, but an indifference to the only things that bring peace. Of tens of thousands it is true that for years they have entirely forgotten God; and if they are returning to Him now, it is only because they are frightened and would

make a pact with God.   They would say to
Him, " Get us out of this and we will do
anything You ask." It is obvious that
should peace be satisfactorily concluded
tomorrow, within a week most of them
would be back in the old slack, pleasure-
loving life of easy complacency from which
all self-discipline is banished and in which
God is completely ignored, and all the wrongs
which cry to God for redress forgotten.   It
would require some new crisis, national or
individual, to hurl them in panic to One
whom they do not really love or understand,
but whom they fear, who they believe has
magic power, and who, if only He could
be prevailed upon by their momentary and
sycophantic appeals, would magically hold
up the law of cause and effect and stay the
evil which years of selfishness have brought
to their hearts and homes.

That this is no exaggeration was seen in
September 1938, when the horror of war was
very close. We let Czecho-Slovakia pay
the price of our peace then, and in the main
we sat back and sleepily watched the crucifixion of a people. A few good souls were
stirred to the depths, but the nation was

not spiritually awakened. It only stirred in its sleep.

But the godly cannot condemn the pagan for bringing all this trouble to the world, for we who do believe in God have ourselves made grim mistakes.

It seems to me that there are two ways of believing in God, a right way and a wrong way, and that we have persistently taken the wrong way. The right way is the attitude which seeks to know God's will and then mobilises all human endeavour in the attempt to carry it out. The wrong way is to outline a human programme, often a valuable and apparently progressive one, put all our energies into working it out, and call on God to bless it.

One way—the right one—says to God, " What wilt Thou have me do ? " and when the answer is clear, puts forth the maximum effort to achieve it. The other way—the wrong way—is that which says, " This is what I am going to do. I hope You will approve, because if anything goes wrong I shall count on You to get me out of the muddle ; and if You don't I shall lose faith in You altogether, or else ask plaintively how a Being calling Himself omnipotent and good can possibly allow such a disaster."

The right way would involve a day of prayer when some projected policy was put before the nation for consideration. The wrong way—though admittedly far better than no recognition of God at all—is to call on Him to get us out of the mess when our unguided human plans have failed.

We reminded ourselves in the first chapter of the immense achievements of man. Although he has forgotten that every human discovery is a divine revelation and that he would have discovered nothing had not God revealed it, yet the inventiveness, ingenuity and resourcefulness are worthy of high praise.

What makes one sick with disappointment is that man's inventiveness was not dedicated at the start to man's highest well-being. We can spend many millions a day on defending ourselves from German aggression and can keep it up. But there is not one social evil that curses our land which, if millions a day were spent on its removal, and if all men's resourcefulness were brought to deal with it, would not disappear in a few months.

Let your mind for just a moment imagine aeroplanes bringing Christ's new way of life to scattered Arab tribes so laboriously and inadequately served by missionaries, under-staffed, underpaid and numerically inadequate. Think of India's seventy million outcastes getting medical and educational services from air-borne doctors and teachers so that infant mortality—now 50 per cent.—and illiteracy—now 94 per cent.—might be improved. What glorious visions thrill the mind which imagines man's brilliant achievements dedicated to man's needs and God's purposes!

But our so-called belief in God has—with some exceptions—only involved following our own plans and then calling on Him to bless them. That is not really belief in God. In Swinburne's line, it has been rather a case of:

" Glory to man in the highest, for man is the master of things."

The fact that this war has meant for many a *spiritual* collapse shows that the real " God " we believed in was collective man.

We had so trusted man's ability, that when man failed we had no other God to fall back on. Man's helplessness then became "God's" defeat, and spiritual collapse followed. The fact is we have never trusted the true God at all.

We have become intoxicated with human ability. We are obsessed by what we have miscalled progress. We have bowed God out at the wings and told Him we can run the play just as well, if not better, without Him. Man has dominated the stage. And the result is hell. At the end of the last war we said, " Now we have cleaned up the world, we will build it afresh." And we have come to a worse hell than ever. The fathers who fought in the war to end war watch their sons going to a hell ten times worse than the last.

Surely Humanism—the damnable doctrine that within man reside all the forces which he needs in order to achieve his worthiest purposes—will be an unwept casualty in this war !

One is sometimes moved to anger by the situation and sometimes to pity : anger that man's insufferable conceit should go

to such lengths, and then pity at Bertrand
Russell's picture of the " soul left to struggle
alone against the whole weight of a universe
that cares nothing for its hopes and fears ".
Our Faith in man is broken, and if humanism was our religion and man our god, then
our collapse is complete.

We need God so desperately, firstly because when we see life truly we know that
His glory is man's first duty and highest
aim, but also so that, dedicating to Him the
abilities He lends to man, we may make sure
that they do not lead us to a worse hell than
we should have made without them.   (And
bows and arrows and spears could not
possibly bring the suffering which poison
gas, flame-throwers, and bombing 'planes
have brought.) We need Him also sub-
jectively, for only in Him is the power to be
found by which we can do His will.   That
fact has been obscured because the false ideas
of Humanism have coloured even our religion, as widespread secular ideas always do.

Christianity began to be—through an
emphasis on the humanity of Christ, valuable up to a point—a message which could
be summarised thus : " Jesus is the perfect

example of human life. Try to imitate Him." But if the emphasis is all on our trying, we are back in Humanism. I cannot be like Him by trying to be like Him. I can only be like Him in the truest sense if, through His endless grace, He gives Himself to me. The Christian Gospel offers the " power to become ". Only so is it a gospel—good news—at all. It doesn't say, " Here is an example, copy it," for then all the emphasis is on my power to do so, to concentrate, to apply myself to the mighty task. Christianity says, " Here is a Friend, open your heart to Him, for He can do for you and in you and with you something that is now beyond you." " Apart from Me ye can do nothing," said Jesus. " In Him that strengtheneth me ", said St. Paul, " I am able for anything."

We see then how important it is to believe in God in the right way : to think of God not as a benign Deity, rather remote, frowning on our sins and smiling upon our little human efforts, but as a Spiritual Force of immense potency—so that we must use the word Omnipotent—decreeing that He will only work in many matters through human agency, but longing for that co-operation, against which man, in the pride of his paltry achievement, shuts his heart, but by which man, now humiliated by war and suffering and trouble, may, please God, still enter, and reach not only blessedness for himself, but make the kind of world in which all men and women and children could be happy and in which they could all share the wealth of God's providence and loving care.

Frankly I see no hope, either nationally or individually, save in an awakening on man's part to God's eternal offer.

Nationally we need to see world brotherhood practised. But why on earth should I take the trouble to think in terms of the world at all, and not just in terms of my own private ends, unless I share the vision of God's purposes, realise that He loves every member of His human family and has a plan for every life? And since I would not raise my eyes from my own interests to see His world, perhaps the sufferings brought so close to us—and coming daily closer—will be the lash in God's hand to whip me into seeing that I ought to have cared about Abyssinians and Czechs and Chinese, years ago, for I *must* be made to realise that God loves all His children and cannot save His world or bring His plans to fruition until *all* His children learn to live together in love. If we had shared this view—indeed, if we had only had more practical common sense —we should have done what Mr. Winston Churchill advised after the last war : we should have sent food in shiploads to starving Germany after the Armistice and worked out a plan to conserve the fine qualities of a great people, and not left them to allow a foul system to enslave them because it seemed to them the only way to the recovery of national self-respect and the cure of a morbid inferiority-complex which defeat inevitably set up.

Isn't it obvious that we need *God's* vision of the world and His power to bring it to pass ? If *anything* else could make it the place God means it to be, it would have been done long ago. If power politics could do it, Germany would be Paradise and her example followed. Instead, the Nazis are dreaded. They have filled Europe with refugees fleeing from their terror. If political theories based on equality " worked ", the Russian programme would have met the case, yet no one thinks Russia has found the key to happiness, least of all the Russians. If brains or words could bring world-happiness, the millennium would be here. Discovery followed discovery, conference followed conference. Never was this old world so full of culture and cleverness and scientific ingenuity, but all man's proud discoveries and wonderful ideas smash on the same rock, SIN, or, if you hate theological terms, selfishness, for they are the same thing. And where is deliverance save in a new ethic, a new vision, and, above all, a new power to make the dream come true? The stark truth is that on every new level of achievement man remains a sinner and uses his cleverness for selfish ends.

How many times have we read the words, " Given good-will there is no reason why our plans should not succeed in establishing peace in Europe " ! But there wasn't enough good-will. And why *should* I have good-will to another unless I see him also as a son of God, a brother for whom Christ died, a co-worker with me for a world good, and all of us co-workers with God? Only so can I be delivered from that accursed emphasis on " I " and " My " (*my* self, *my* group, *my* party, *my* country), into the vision which sees no nation but humanity, and no king but God.

When I turn to the problem of the individual it is the same. We are cursed by what Karl Barth calls Titanism—that absurd idea that we can lift ourselves by our own shoe-strings and become the kind of men we want to be, either for the world task which awaits us, or for the inner victory which must precede it. How many of us have felt with Paul, " I do not act as I want to act; on the contrary, I do what I detest . . . *The wish is there but not the power of doing what is right*. I cannot be good as I want to be, and I do wrong against my own wishes. . . . I want to do right, but wrong is all I can manage. . . . Miserable wretch that I am ! Who will rescue me from this body of death ? "   How few of us go on with Paul to add, " God will ! Thanks be to Him through Jesus Christ our Lord ".[1]

There is no denial of the value and power of the will there. It must be exercised to

[1] Rom. 7[15-25] (Moffatt).

open the door to God and keep it open.
But it is an expression of the vital truth,
the forgetting of which brings us so much
failure and suffering, that the *power to
become* is of God alone.

What profound truth there is in the old
story of the young man who went to his
minister and said, " What can I do to get
peace ? "   " Young man," said the minister,
" you are too late."   " What ! " said the
youth, " do you mean I am too late to be
saved ? "   " Oh no, not that," came the
reply; " but you are too late to do anything. Jesus did everything that needed
to be done centuries ago."

We need this truth desperately. The day
of national prayer shows so clearly that
men reach a point when they realise—
dimly, it may be, fearfully, and with often a
false picture of God in their minds—that
God matters more than anything else in the
world. Yet still we believe in God in the
wrong way. We submit our programme to
Him and say, " I hope You will approve."
So our hearts are still troubled, and we go
on our hectic way unblessed, unable, with
all our weary quests, to find peace.

Let us begin to believe in God in the right way. After all, if we consulted a human friend for whom we had a great veneration and respect because of his knowledge and experience and wisdom and power, we shouldn't say, " This is what I'm going to do, and I want your approval." We should say, " What would you advise me to do ? "

When we come to God like that we are coming to the Infinitely Wise and Loving and Strong, and we are coming, not to ask His approval of *our* plans, but that we may co-operate with Him in His glorious work. When we say to Him, " What wilt Thou have me to do ? " He will show us the next step. If what we call disaster overtakes us, it will be all right. We are in His hands. What happens to us then will be His care. And He can bring us through, for nothing can finally defeat Him. *Then* our hearts will not be troubled. We shall believe in God.

Let us begin with peace in our own hearts, and work in every way open to us for peace in the world, remembering that, both within and without, the peace of God can only be built up and established on God's plan, by God's men, in God's way, for God's glory.

F

CHAPTER FOUR

FAITH MUST KEEP HER EYES ON GOD

THE OTHER DAY, WHEN I HAD BEEN LISTEN-
ing to too much " news " and reading the
newspaper so assiduously that my horizon
was limited to this world, I found a message
of great strengthening for my own soul from
two passages in the Scriptures, written down
by prophets whose people were under the
fear of the threat of armed force. In the
messages of both these men there is no
reference whatever to the armed force !

Here are the two passages. The first is
in Isaiah xl, and runs like this : " Comfort
ye, comfort ye my people, saith your God.
Speak ye comfortably to Jerusalem [literally,
" to the heart of Jerusalem "], and cry unto
her, that her warfare is accomplished, that
her iniquity is pardoned : for she hath
received of the Lord's hand double for all

her sins.[1] The voice of him that crieth in the wilderness, Prepare ye the way of the Lord, make straight in the desert a highway for our God. Every valley shall be exalted, and every mountain and hill shall be made low; and the crooked shall be made straight, and the rough places plain : And the glory of the Lord shall be revealed, and all flesh shall see it together; for the mouth of the Lord hath spoken it . . . Say unto the cities of Judah, Behold your God ! "

[1] I have read that in Isaiah's day if a man became insolvent the list of all his liabilities was written on a parchment and nailed up, with a nail at the top and another at the bottom, in some public place. If a rich friend saw this humiliating document he would sometimes take out the bottom nail, double the parchment in two, write his name across the folded document and drive the bottom nail in again next the top nail, securing the parchment in this folded form. His signature meant that he would be responsible for his friend's debts. I have wondered whether this practice is referred to in this passage. The grim account of our sins is doubled up and God's name written across it. One is reminded of the book which recorded the taxes to be exacted from each town and village in France. The page headed Domremy is said to be doubled back, and across the folded portion one finds the words written—" Free for the Maid's Sake ".

Turn to the second passage. Five hundred years afterwards we find John the Baptist, living at a time when the men he loved most were ground down under the heel of the Roman tyranny, bringing the message of the good news about Jesus in these words : " As it is written in the Prophets, behold I send my messenger before Thy face, which shall prepare Thy way before Thee. The voice of one crying in the wilderness, Prepare ye the way of the Lord, make His paths straight." John, we remember, was baptising in Jordan and inviting people to repent, confessing their sins (Mark i. 2–4).

Here we are in London in 1940, in real and quite natural fear from armed force. Invasion, we are told, may come. Indeed, at the time of writing, it comes through the air every night. If I could write about Hitler and Mussolini and how they should be dealt with, I am quite sure that you would read my words eagerly. But I feel equally sure that the word of the Lord for His people today is not a word about Hitler or Mussolini, any more than in Isaiah's day it was a word about

Nebuchadnezzar and in John the Baptist's day a word about Pilate, or Cæsar.

What we need to say to one another is a word about God. " Behold your God ! " What an important message that is ! Look at God ! God is working for righteousness all the time, and He is asking us, apart from all that we do from the motive of patriotism, to put away our sins, to become sensitive to Him, and thus to prepare His way before Him.

Now let us look at the ancient pictures a little more closely. Nebuchadnezzar sacked Jerusalem in 586 B.C., and the words from Isaiah were probably written down about forty years afterwards. I wonder how those words were received at the time ! Jerusalem was in ruins, inhabited by a destitute and wretched population. A great many people had been taken right across the desert to Babylon to live in exile. You can imagine them there in Babylon—just a small group of people compared with the Babylonians around them, a little better fed than their brothers in Jerusalem, but very unhappy and lonely, moaning their sad lament, " How can we sing the Lord's song in a strange land ? " And all around them were the signs of the might of the civilisation of Babylon. Babylon was almost a synonym for power. " Great is Babylon the mighty ! " was a slogan.

It must have seemed to those Jews that they were watching the end of Jewish history, and they would have listened eagerly if someone had given them a message as to how they could escape from Nebuchadnezzar and restore the greatness of Jerusalem. Supposing that you and I could have been amongst them. Supposing that we could have spoken—shall we say ?—to the Prime Minister of Babylon on the steps of the Town Hall ! If we had asked him what, in his opinion, would become of the Jewish remnants in the midst of this mighty city, I think he would merely have shrugged his shoulders and said that their day was done, that they would remain there indefinitely and probably become completely absorbed in the life that was around them.

One lovely evening I rode with a friend on horseback across the desert towards Babylon. As the sun went down in golden splendour we ate our evening meal on the sands of the desert. We waited until the moon rose, and then, in the moonlight, we guided our horses amongst the ruins of this ancient civilisation. You may still wander up and down the old streets, and if you are a certain kind of person you may secrete a brick from Nebuchadnezzar's ancient palace and bring it home with you ! In the centre of the city you will find an obscene statue of a woman and some animal, but, apart from references in literature and these old excavated stones, how little Babylon has meant to the life of the world since !

Yet here in London, 2500 years afterwards, we are comforting one another by reading the inspired words of the despised leader of a little group of Jews in the heart of that mighty civilisation. Babylon is, to use Tennyson's words,

> Blown about the desert dust
> And sealed within the iron hills.

But all that the life of the Jews meant as the people of God, to whom God was a living Reality, is still like a stream of sweet, fresh water in a desert, bringing life to the thirsty souls of men.

Now turn for a moment to the other ancient picture. Here is John the Baptist out in the wilds all those years afterwards. He is dressed only in skins, and living on the simple sustenance of the desert. All around him he finds a people seething with a desire to rebel against the tyranny of a Dictator. If only John had told them how to overthrow the yoke of Rome, how they would have listened to him and acted upon his words! His wild eloquence is such that the message he does bring compels their attention, but he is talking about sins and repentance. He is telling them to watch God and be sensitive to God, and asking them to prepare, not the way of a deliverer from Rome's tyranny, but the way of the Lord.

We know now that if the Jews had had the kind of Messiah they wanted, the kind of person they may have imagined John was talking about, we should certainly never have heard of him. It is rather a striking comment on the might of Rome that most people would never have heard of Pilate at all save for his distinguished Prisoner.

The mighty dictatorship that crushed the
people with such ruthless oppression in those
days that they groaned under the tyranny,
would hardly have been heard of but for
Jesus. How popular would have been a
message that showed a way of escape from
Rome, or the overthrow of Rome, and yet
how little it would have meant today !

I think that already you will have picked
up a clue to the message I want to express.
Many, at the present moment, would listen
eagerly to a voice that told them how
successfully to win the war, how to smash
Hitler, and how to stop Mussolini. That is
the business of the Government. But the
minister of Christ must appeal to Christian
people to be awake to a different kind of
message, but one which may have a far
greater significance in the end, and that is
this same old message : " Watch God. Be
sensitive to God. Behold your God ! And,
in order that you may see Him more clearly,
put away your sins in order that you may
prepare His way."

I want to offer you three truths about
God which have brought to my own mind a

sense of peace amid all the troubles through which we are passing.[1]

As we watch God let us realise—

First, that God is greater than His world.

Second, that God works through His world.

Third, that God suffers with His world.

It is not easy to find a single illustration, for the nature of God is so august that we find when we emphasise one aspect of it we almost deny another. But it may help some to think of a man in relation to his own hand. (1) He is greater than it, transcendent above it, and would exist if he lost it. So is God in relation to His world. (2) A man uses his hand, works with it, expresses himself by it. So does God in relation to His world. (3) A man suffers if his hand is injured, feels by means of it, is sensitive to anything which wounds it. So is God in relation to His world of men and women.

[1] The substance of what follows in this chapter was broadcast over the wireless and is reproduced by the kindness of the B.B.C.

Let us take these three thoughts and look at them.

I

The transcendence of God. Faith can maintain her true perspective by looking away from life's troubles to the greatness of God.

When I am tempted to think that God is incapable of managing His world, that He has let it get into a hopeless mess, and that I could have done much better if I had been God, I am brought back to sanity by the thought of a tiny spider crawling up one of the pillars outside the City Temple. Perhaps his spidery mind is beset with terrific anxiety because he has somehow to negotiate one of the tiny holes in the stone or a crack in the mortar. If he had sufficient thinking apparatus—which he has not— his anxiety and sense of insecurity would be increased a thousandfold. What possible picture could he have in his mind of the architecture of a single pillar, far less the architecture of the City Temple, and less still the purpose for which the City Temple was built and exists? What possible clue

could he have to the immense spiritual
energies which have been sent out into the
world from this building through its long
history? And could that spider have any
idea at all of the architecture of London
and of the life of the vast metropolis? I
do not think I am exaggerating when I say
that we are very much like that spider.
We may know pretty well our own little
haunts and the things that happen around
them, but the immensity of God it is
impossible to exaggerate. We do not even
know very much about our own planet, and
as for its spiritual significance—as for God's
spiritual plans throughout the whole of His
vast universe—we can only pick up the
merest guess. Really the amazing thing is
that such insignificant creatures as ourselves should even have enough of a hint
on which to base reason, and not just be
limited to blind faith, or, indeed, utter
despair.

In a true sense it is only because God *is*
God, that He is big enough to allow human
free-will to lead to such awful calamities as
those of which the world is full, and yet
know that ultimately He can so handle the

situation as to bring out of chaos the achievement of His purpose with nothing of final value ultimately lost. Of this—as far as we can glimpse it in a human picture—the Cross is the supreme illustration.

It is impossible to believe that the temporary evil engendered by one or two nations can overthrow the plans of a transcendent God.

I held in my hands recently a piece of shrapnel which had made a hole in my roof and the remains of an incendiary bomb which burnt itself out near my front door. I asked a friend whether he believed that those and similar bits of metal, mined originally from God's own earth, or even the biggest size in bombs, could really defeat the plans of the Architect of this Universe. In spite of all the horror, we knew that *that* wasn't true. We found a bit of courage in getting our perspective corrected by a thought of the greatness of God.

II

But look at a second truth. *God is working in and through His world.*

Obviously God must not do for us what we can do for ourselves, but He works with us in endless co-operation. Behind almost all human enterprise there has been something given, something demanded. We could take almost any valuable discovery as an illustration. Something to be discovered is given, and the brain to discover it. But something is demanded : the energy and devotion and patience to make the discovery and use it. A surgical instrument is an illustration which occurs to one. God hid the iron in the hills. That is given. But man must toil to find it, make steel from it, adapt it, fashion it and use it cleverly in the service of humanity.

How true are the words, " Without God, we cannot ; without us, God will not " ! Apply them to the world situation. To have prevented the possibility of this war, God would have had to rob man of the richest treasure hidden in his heart, that which makes him man—his free will. Those who want God to stop the power of a dictator are frequently found to be praying that God would become one Himself. They pray that God would stop war without asking just at what point they want the Divine Dictator to act. To prevent the *possibility* of war God could not have created men free at all.

No! Having given men freedom and set them in families and nations, He is working out a plan for their unity and their final development as beings fit for perfect communion with Himself. But because we don't follow the plan, we deduce that it is meaningless, forgetting that no wise man judges a plot on the stage a few seconds after the curtain has gone up. That is what we tend to do. We need the rebuke of Francis Quarles.

> My soul sit thou a patient looker-on,
> Judge not the play before the play is done,
> Her plot hath many changes, every day
> Speaks a new scene; the last act crowns the play.

Let us take the illustration of the stage a little further. You have probably been to the theatre when, in the course of the play, there has at some time been on the stage a great crowd of people. Perhaps even a battle is raging on the stage, but you are not obsessed by the battle, because you are watching the hero and the heroine. The battle and the noise and the tumult are, as it were, a background, throwing up what is of far greater interest to the careful watcher : the activity of the central figures. If you happened to walk through the theatre when the battle scene was raging on the stage, you might carelessly look towards it and remark that evidently the whole play was concerned with a great battle. But those who have watched the play right through realise that, although the battle is significant enough, noisy and tumultuous enough, it is really very much of a side-show compared with the action of the hero and heroine.

We must not let our minds be obsessed by the war, even though it seems to be tumultuous and noisy enough to fill heaven and earth. If I may so put it thus reverently, God is playing a much bigger game than appears. The plot which is being worked out on this noisy stage is a plot of which God is the Hero. I am not making a little thing of the war and the brave sacrifices of so many thousands of people. I am certainly far from feeling callous concerning their suffering. I see too much of it every day. But when we have said all that, we simply must not let our minds become so obsessed by the terror and fury of what is, after all, stage scenery, so that we forget that GOD is at work. "Say unto the cities of Judah, Behold your God!" He is not responsible for the stage-setting, but He is certainly not crowded off the stage by it. Let us put away our sins so that we may be sensitive to God; let us watch God and co-operate, wherever we can, with Him. Let us not be as those who might pass through the world and see merely a world at war, and let us never judge a play until the curtain comes down at the end. By the time that happens we shall know that God is the Hero, and that "the play's the thing", not the setting. And the play that God is working out in His world is something far bigger than either our military victory or defeat. The stage is set for the eternal purposes of God. And he who has a pure heart, who is trying to put away his sins, who is quietly trustful and sensitive to the movement of God's spirit; he who knows how to listen to the voice of God and knows the difference between the noise of an earthquake and the still, small voice, will not only be able to

G

comfort himself, but others too; and he will be able to do a far greater thing than either : he will be able to prepare the way of the Lord and play his part in the working out of that drama which we sometimes call the redemption of the world.

The attitude of the early Christians to persecution shows us the way. We can have very little conception of what it must have been to undergo persecution in the time of Nero. The very fact of the brave witness of the early Christians to their faith draws the attention of the historic observer away from the horrors which those Christians underwent. When we think of the persecutions, we think less of the horror and barbarity than we do of the witness. What a tribute to those early Christians that fact is ! But I suppose even the horrors of a German concentration camp were exceeded when girls were stripped naked and thrown into the arena to the lions; men crucified upside down for a jest; women tied on the horns of maddened oxen to make a Roman holiday; the bodies of youths and maidens covered with pitch to be set on fire to illuminate Nero's garden at night. Yet if such a word can be used, the obsession of the early Christians was with Christ, never with Rome.[1] They appear not to have held big mass meetings to decide what could be done about Nero. In Pliny's phrase, " They sang hymns to Christ as God." And just as Pilate is now forgotten, save that he happened to be on the stage at the same time as Jesus, so Nero is all but forgotten, save that he happened to be a horrible part of the stage scenery when the drama which concerned the birth of the Church was being worked out. In those days Paul was a little, crippled, despised tent-maker with certain powers of oratory, and Nero the mighty was on the throne; but now, as has been observed, a significant thing has happened, for people call their dogs " Nero " and they call their sons " Paul."

Certainly if we become obsessed by the war we shall lose all sense of proportion; we may be in despair; we shall probably become bitter. If we lose the war we shall

[1] Cf. the tone of the first epistle of St. Peter written in A.D. 65 to Christians enduring Nero's persecution and the oppression of a totalitarian state.

think it is the end of everything, and if we win the war we shall be tempted to give way to reprisal and revenge and make a good peace impossible. If, on the other hand, our minds keep the central place of the stage for the activity of God, then we shall, if we think it right, resist the enemy in whatever ways are open to us with a minimum of horror and outrage of human nature; but when the dreadful days are over and peace is again possible, we shall be ready so to prepare the way of the Lord that He may take His rightful place in the destinies of the nations. Thus a constructive peace may be built up which is stable because it has its basis in the eternal things that nothing can move.

III

But let us not forget our third truth, *that God is sensitive to all that wounds His world.* He is immanent in it, and wherever its harmony is broken He Himself suffers from the disharmony. Never think of God as remote from human suffering as a man who might sit on a wall and watch ants struggling in the dust below his feet. He is *in* it all, suffering, not physical agony, but a spiritual anguish far greater and too poignant for us to guess.

If Mencius, in regard to the dykes in China which held back the water, could say, " I feel responsible for every man who drowns in China ", what does an infinite and loving God, who is immanent in every life, feel about those who suffer either in mind or body ? If a Chinese patient could say of a beloved doctor, " He took my sickness into his own heart ",[1] then are we surprised to hear a prophet crying out, " In all our afflictions He was afflicted . . . in His love and in His pity He redeemed us ; and He bare us and carried us all the days of old. . . . He bare the sin of many " ? He is still " wounded for our transgressions, bruised for our iniquities ; the chastisement of our peace is upon Him ; and with His stripes we are healed ". " I do not ask the wounded person how he feels," said Walt Whitman in a sentence of amazing insight, " I myself become the wounded person."

[1] " Christ and Human Suffering " (Dr. Stanley Jones), p. 176.

If your little child suffers, and to comfort him you press him to your breast and hold him tightly to you, you do so because, if it were possible, you would draw him within yourself and bear his pain. You would make his little, suffering personality an extension of your own. God has done that. He *is* immanent, and suffers more than we do, because His capacity for feeling is greater, His love deeper, His horror of sin more intense. God is the greatest casualty in this or any war, and while we are naturally concerned with our own troubles, He bears those of Finland and Poland and China and Spain and Abyssinia, and Norway and Holland and Belgium and France and Greece, and has always carried the whole world's burdens. The problem is no different because it has been brought nearer to *us*.

Do not therefore ask petulantly, " Why does God let this happen? " Finish the question and say, "Why does God let this happen to Himself? "

It is an awesome thought, but attested by the Incarnation and sufferings of Christ, that God has delivered Himself in a sense into our hands. Our own sympathy with

others, never so identified with them as if
we were immanent in them, is restrained by
our indifference, our selfishness, our sheer
exhaustion. But He is never indifferent,
never selfish and cannot be exhausted.
Truly " the Lamb was slain from the
foundation of the world ".

How we misunderstand God ! To keep
the figure of the stage it seems oddly
illogical that man, instead of playing his
part on the stage by faithfully interpreting
in life the mind of the Author of the plot,
should act as though he had had no instructions as to what to do and say, and then
curse the Author because the play was not
running smoothly.

Just as logically, I might try to climb the
Matterhorn, neglecting entirely the advice of
the guide, and then, having fallen to the
bottom of a precipice, curse the guide for
not conducting the adventure more successfully, or explain to my fellow-sufferers that
I did not believe the guide knew better than
I did. Almost every day I hear someone
declare that he cannot believe in God any
longer, or that no good God would allow
such evil to happen. But humanity is like

a foolish mountaineer who, careless of all that past history can teach, seeks to climb the heights of self-realisation in defiance of all that God is eager to teach him about the only way in which such heights can be attained.

So we must leave the matter. Let me repeat the threefold thought. (1) God is infinitely greater than His universe. It is not so true to say that He can put the wrong right, as to say that He can even use wrong in His cause, as He used the Cross on which cruel men crucified the Holiest among them. God is adequate to every situation. We need not think the universe has got out of His control. Nothing would be allowed to happen which God could not ultimately use, even though as yet we cannot see how.

(2) God is working out a purpose, vast, and, to our minds, so complicated that it looks a hopeless tangle; but He asks our quiet, loving, trustful co-operation, to do the best we know, and leave the responsibility of results to Him. Has it struck you that the extent of the tangle is a measure of His power, a challenge which His omnipotence can meet?

(3) God is not remote and removed from our sorrow and pain. Because He is immanent in His world, and because infinite love means an infinite capacity for pain, He not only shares it, but bears by far the greater portion Himself. Yet there is joy at the heart of the Universe, for ultimately the price paid will not have been too great to buy the world that shall be. That is what redemption means.

So let us have more than courage. Courage is fine, but it can remain quite pagan, and is consistent even with hopelessness.[1] Let us have faith : " This is the victory . . . even our faith "; faith to believe that the great Architect has planned something vast, but very beautiful, from this pathetic, lowly, glorious thing called human life. If the Architect showed us the plans in His eternal mind we could not understand. If He explained, we could not understand the explanation. It is not necessary that we should. It is only

---

[1] I have worked out the thought that we need more than courage in a small pamphlet published by the English Universities Press, " Is It Courage We Need ? " (6d.).

necessary to believe that there *is* a plan, that there *is* an explanation.

And I get confidence, not from the plans, most of which are too vast for my little comprehension, but from the Architect's face. " All things were made through Him," said the Author of the Fourth Gospel,[1] " In Him all things hold together," said St. Paul.[2] And again, " It is God who said, Light shall shine out of darkness, who shined in our hearts, to give the light of the knowledge of the glory of God in the face of Jesus Christ."[3]   In the glimpse I get of Jesus from the Gospels, from my poor little faith, and, above all, from lives that reflect His glory, I get the assurance I want. The face of Jesus tells me that God is living, loving, working, suffering, but triumphant at last. Faith must keep her eyes on God. So let me keep my eyes on the face of Jesus Christ, who, nailed to a Cross, still called God, " Father ".   " We see not yet all things subjected to Him . . . but we behold . . .

[1] John 1³ (R.V. marg.).
[2] Col. 1¹⁷ (R.V. marg.).
[3] 2 Cor. 4⁶.

Jesus, . . . crowned with glory and honour." [1]   Let us be content to try to do our bit in the world, and trust Him for the rest.   Duty is for man.   Destiny for God.   Confidently and trustfully we can lift up to One who is both the Architect of the Universe and our Loving Father all the things that defeat and depress us.   There is forgiveness there, and joy and peace. There, and I think there only, the mind can find a sense of victory.   " This is the victory that overcometh, even our faith."

[1] Heb. 2[9].

CHAPTER FIVE

FAITH MISUNDERSTOOD

LET US, IN THIS CHAPTER, DISCUSS SOME things which faith in God does *not* mean.

I

A young lady recently asked me whether showing signs of nervousness and fear during an air-raid and of tension during these diffi-cult days meant that one's faith in God was defective. Was she " letting Christ down " ?

It is most important to answer " No ".

Fear is a perfectly normal reaction of the human mechanism. In another place [1] I have tried to show that fear is a healthy reaction against danger, and if it had not been instinctive, the human level would never have been reached in man's develop-

[1] " Psychology and Life," p. 249 (Hodder & Stoughton).

ment. Fear makes for safety—as when we cross a street full of traffic. It makes for efficiency—as when the chemist makes up a prescription. It makes for righteousness —as when we fear the consequences of evil. It is the basis of worship, for awe is sub-blimated fear. It is the basis of courage, for courage is the right reaction to a fear-causing situation. Without fear there could be no such thing as courage.

We must not therefore condemn ourselves for feeling fear, though we must watch that fear does not drive us to infect others, run away, or do anything unworthy.

Symptoms of fear may show themselves—rigors, pallor, trembling, fainting and so on; they are no occasion for shame, and may as really measure courage as its opposite, for the sensitive, imaginative person who sees farther into the fear-causing situation, and yet will not run away though he trembles violently, shows more courage than he who never realised or imagined all there was to be feared.

Again, experiences of early childhood, temperament, unconscious complexes and inhibitions all play their part in determining what symptoms of fear we show, so that we cannot judge others or assess our own courage merely in terms of symptoms.

It should be added that at a time of great strain it is usually the so-called neurotic who stands up to the test best, and those who are stolid extraverts who often get knocked out. Several nurses I have consulted agree here. Months ago, when the wailing siren was a new and rather frightening experience, I was told by a patient in a hospital for nervous diseases that when the alarm sounded, a neurotic patient walked calmly downstairs to an air-raid shelter showing no signs of fear, and, being found there, was told by a doctor that she was a stretcher case, and ordered to go up again so as to be *carried* down! According to my informant the doctor who gave the order and the attendants whose duty it was to carry the stretcher seemed almost incapacitated through fear. I suppose the neurotic is so used to adapting himself to fear-causing situations that he can do so in an emergency better than the person who boasts he has never " felt fear in his life ". The new, big demand knocks him over.

Thus the reed which bends to every wind, bows before the gale and quickly recovers. The oak and the elm have much greater resistance, but if this is overcome they cannot make adjustment. They are blown down.

So never feel that your faith in God is tested by physical or nervous symptoms of fear. Jesus was sweating blood in Gethsemane, but who would say He had no courage or that He was a spiritual casualty? One might become in war-time a physical or psychological casualty through fear—especially, for example, if modern experiences lit up some hidden complex or revived hideous memories of the last war—yet one's faith in God would not thereby be denied.

Faith in God does mean that there will be no *spiritual* collapse. You will know, whatever happens, that God is still in charge of His world, that His values will ultimately triumph, that in spite of any appearances He cannot be defeated, and that you and your dear ones are still in His loving care and will win through at last to the fulfilment of His purposes. In a word, faith will save you from the awful mental condition which I have called meaninglessness, from being a spiritual casualty. "This is the victory that overcometh, even our faith."

II

Faith in God does not mean an insurance against calamity for yourself or your dear ones. That ought not to need saying, and yet in so many cases men say, "I prayed for my boy, and now he is missing or killed. I shan't believe in God any more."

It is strange that men cannot see that with human free-will uncoerced; with human ignorance not magically exchanged for knowledge, or human folly for wisdom; with every individual bound up with others, gaining and losing from them, there must remain the possibility of evil done to *our* dear ones as well as anyone else's, and that if religion were a magic cloak which we could throw over our loved ones, everyone would adopt it, not out of love for God, but as they would adopt any other safety device, and religion would lose its nature and faith its character.

A. A. Milne tells [1] of a quiet boy in his
battalion in the last war whose only brother
had been killed.   To his mother the boy
was very precious, and, laugh or cry as you
will, she bought him an undergarment of
chain mail such as had been worn in the
Middle Ages to guard against unfriendly
daggers.   It was supposed to guard him
against a bayonet-thrust or a fragment of
shell.   He was much embarrassed by the
gift, but, to please his mother, he took it
to France with him.   He asked Milne's
advice, timidly, pathetically.   He had promised his mother, but, on the other hand,
it seemed unsporting, something not quite
done.   Milne told him to wear it and tell
his mother he was wearing it and how safe
it made him feel and how certain of coming
back to her.   " I don't know whether he
took my advice," says Mr. Milne.   " Anyway, it didn't matter, for on the evening
when we first came within reach of the
battle-zone, just as he was settling down
to his tea, a crump came over and blew
him to pieces."

[1] " Peace with Honour ", A. A. Milne, p. 55
(Methuen).

H

No, we cannot, either by a suit of mail or an earnest prayer, save our dear ones from physical danger, and although I pray for the physical safety of those I love—and feel justified in doing so, for a child cannot keep from his Father the deep desires of his heart—I admire a young woman who recently said concerning her soldier-lover, " I don't pray for his safety, only that he may remain brave and unstained and do his job. He must take the risks the others take."

In olden days men *did* believe that religion was a safety device, as some of the Psalms show. " A thousand shall fall at thy side and ten thousand at thy right hand but it shall not come nigh thee." [1] To put it bluntly, that is untrue, unless we spiritualise it, which is not what the Psalmist meant. But Jesus never promised it. He said to *His* dear ones, " Men will hate you and persecute you and drive you from city to city and kill you, thinking they do God service . . . and he that endureth to the end shall be saved." [2]

---

[1] Psalm 91⁷.   [2] Matt. 24⁹; Mark 13⁹; Matt. 10²².

He is saved surely in the sense that he finds he has fulfilled God's plan after all, although it looked as though the forces arrayed against him had it all their own way. He is saved from meaninglessness in life and maintained throughout in a sense of inward peace and security. God's promise is not that if we believe in Him we shall be delivered *from* the waters. It is greater than that. It is that when we pass through them, He will be there too.[1] And *all* the waters, including the flood of evil released in the world by Hitlerism, are in the hollow of His hand. In a sense they are His. " All *Thy* waves and *Thy* billows are gone over me." [2] The power to do evil is the power of God. " Thou could'st have no power against me," said Jesus to Pilate, "unless it were given thee from above." [3] Is an omnipotent God finally defeated by a power of evil which is only possible by His own permission? God *is* God because He can make the wrath of men to serve Him. Again and again the Kingdom of God has been ultimately

[1] Isa. 43[2].   [2] Psalm 42[7].
[3] John 19[11].

furthered by means which belong to the kingdom of evil.[1]

III

This brings us to our third thought, that faith in God does not necessarily mean that we shall win this war.   I believe we shall. I certainly hope we shall.   But my faith in God will not be broken if we don't. After all, my faith in God was not shattered when Poland was ravaged.   Why should it be shattered if England suffer?   Poland means as much to the Pole as Britain does to me.

God might be able to do more with a defeated nation that was penitent than with a victorious nation that was aggressive.   A really penitent nation might turn to God, and, even if dominated by cruelty, might be the leaven which God could use to make a new Europe.   If war ended tomorrow to our advantage, a proud, victorious nation might slip back at once to paganism,

[1] This point I have worked out in " Thinking Aloud in War-time ", p. 129 (Hodder & Stoughton).

materialism and international selfishness, and show such vindictive pride—even claiming God on her side—that the cause of true religion would not necessarily be served even by victory as much as it might be served through defeat. Defeat can be a very healthy spiritual condition both in men and nations, for, having nothing else to trust in, they may turn to God.

One of the most marvellous messages of the Gospel of Christ, to my mind, is that if we have faith in God we shall find that those things which we call calamities and disasters contribute as much *finally*—and I must emphasise that word—to our blessedness as those things for which we long and pray : success, peace, health, influence and deliverance from bereavement, suffering, poverty and distress.

Evil, of course, is not to be welcomed. It is to be fought and overcome if possible. It may be right to evade evils if they can be evaded honourably. But if they have to be endured, their compulsion for us is God's guarantee that they can minister as much to His goal—which is our blessedness —as what we call His benefits. " With

them that love God, He co-operates, in all
things, for good." [1]

And our final goal *is* blessedness. Neither
victory nor defeat matters as much as that.
God is Spirit and we are spirit, and part of
Him. We function as an extension of His
own Being, and if we were blotted out
wholly and entirely, spirit as well as body,
then God Himself would suffer ultimate
loss—which is impossible. There cannot be
such a thing as annihilation of our being, or
it would be loss of His life. Life may pass
to other forms on other planes, and such a
passing may leave us sorrowful and desolate
for a time. But nothing can destroy spirit
or energy. It only changes its form. " Fear
not them that kill the body and AFTER
THAT have no more that they can do."
Those are the words of Jesus [2]—the greatest
Authority in this realm that the world has
ever known. There is an " after that ",
then. Life goes on.

And the Potter must be allowed control
of the clay. " Then the vessel was marred

---

[1] Prof. C. H. Dodd's translation of Rom. 8[28] in his
Commentary, p. 138 (Hodder & Stoughton).
[2] Luke 12[4].

in the hand of the Potter, so he made it again another vessel as it seemed good to the Potter to make it." [1] And that means the fire. If that fire be one lighted in the world by evil hands for an evil purpose, God may yet use it to purify our nation. And to say that He does so, does not imply that the fire was intended by Him ever to be lighted or that it represents His will.

Faith in God doesn't mean that God will leap out of Heaven and stop causes from bringing their own effects. He may let the effects ensue and save us by the way which costs us and Himself most. He may lead us through the fire. (And if we pass through it, He will be there too.) And fire is, in a way, a compliment to the nature of the faith expected from us. Fire points to gold—not wood.

IV

Faith in God does not mean an easy-going dissociation of ourselves from the heart-breaking sorrow around us. No man who stands away from the great sorrow of our

[1] Jer. 18⁴.

world, steeling his heart to callousness as one who says, " I told you so. Behold the judgment of God," is showing Christ's spirit. We must turn with all our power to remedy the sorrows and calamities of men, but maintaining our faith that God is working against them, through them and in them. Jesus wept over the city, but its utter destruction, which He foretold, would not, even if it had occurred in His lifetime, have made Him lose faith in God.

V

Faith in God does not mean sitting down idly and complacently hoping that all will come right in the end. There is a so-called faith which is little more than health, success and high spirits, and can be almost pagan. Real Christian faith does not function while pagan optimism rules. Real Christian faith begins to shine when man is most ready to acknowledge that he cannot alone reach his goal. God will "make it all right in the end", but only as and when men co-operate with Him and are ready even for evil to be used in His service. What is wanted is that eager sensitiveness to find *His* way and the courage to follow it *even though it leads through the fire of used evil.* The flames of Hell are the fires of redemption. They are never mere retribution, but always cleansing discipline to those who have faith in God. But we must include a consideration of them in our philosophy of life.

I remember a friend of mine, who shrank from the doctrine of Hell, asking Dr. Orchard—who was then a Modernist—whether the thought of Hell might not, in these modern days of enlightenment, be dismissed. Very quietly, with a queer grin, came the answer, " I shouldn't bank on it if I were you." No; we may have caricatured the teaching about Hell, but originally it came from the gentlest lips in the world, the lips of Jesus.

VI

Faith in God does not mean that there will necessarily ever be on earth the kind of Utopia of which men dream. There may be. I often think there will be, but

I find little evidence for it. Says Reinhold Niebuhr, " Most alternatives to the Christian faith are cheap forms of credulity which seek to save life from despair by hoping for and expecting happy consummations in life and history, for which the experience of the ages offers not the slightest verification." [1]   Arnold Toynbee tells us that fourteen out of the twenty-one great civilisations of the earth have perished. The remainder are in a perilous state. Most of them are now at war.   Is there any special reason why ours should survive ? If modern Western civilisation passes away as have passed the ancient civilisations of Babylon, Greece, Rome, Mexico, Egypt and the rest, we shall feel sorry at the collapse of so much that has given us many valuable things, but we shall be saved from despair. We shall be able to bear the thought of such a collapse, for faith in God is a reassurance that if not here, then hereafter, the Kingdom of God will be established.

What faith in God does mean I shall deal with more fully later.   But it does mean a

[1] " Europe's Catastrophe and the Christian Faith ", p. 45 (Nisbet).

worthy *dénouement* of human history either
on this earth or in heaven. It does mean
that this old world, this fraction of the
universe, has not run amok. It isn't out
of His control, neither is any single life
upon it. Though the climax of history
be delayed—and that is man's fault—it
will surely come.

> And not one life shall be destroyed,
> Or cast as rubbish to the void,
> When God hath made the pile complete.

No, not one life, in any of the ravished
countries or in the oceans or Norway's
dark fiords. No brave airman, British
or German, Grecian or Italian, falling out
of the sky can fall out of God's hands. No
little Abyssinian child, scarred for life by
the mustard gas which Italy used to bring
" progress " and " civilisation " to a backward people in the " dark Continent ", is
one moment forgotten by God. No Christian pastor, tortured and sexually assaulted
by the perverts who run German concentration camps will have suffered in vain or
remain unavenged when God closes the
final accounts.

Nothing of value can be finally lost. All

the true values will have their worth, and, what is more, their worthwhileness, vindicated. And nothing we may be called upon to go through would be allowed to come near us if *in itself* it had power to touch our souls. Everything depends on our attitude. And we need not wait for a final consummation to see some of the sin and suffering of life redeemed, for every bit of it can be used, as it were, to buy back from the universe something greater than itself in measure of blessedness for ourselves and benediction for others.

> If I stoop
> Into a dark, tremendous sea of cloud,
> It is but for a time; I press God's lamp
> Close to my breast; its splendour, soon or late,
> Will pierce the gloom : I shall emerge one day.

And, please God, we shall emerge, nationally and individually, not embittered, vindictive, spiritually defeated or blatantly, boastfully victorious, but cleansed, purified, redeemed, to find our goal in blessedness and all our dreams come true in Him who loved us and gave Himself for us that He might bring us *all* to God. " This is the victory that overcometh, even our faith."

CHAPTER SIX

FAITH'S TRIUMPHANT DECLARATIONS

WE NEED BADLY TODAY THE VICTORIOUS *certainty* of faith. How that note rings down the ages through the Bible and beyond! From Job, a drama going back to nearly 500 B.C., come these words: " I *know* that my Vindicator liveth." [1] " I *know* that Thou canst do all things and that no purpose of Thine can be restrained." [2] From St. Paul come the words: " We *know* [3] that all things work together for good." " I *know* Whom I have believed." [4]

If the Biblical writings had been continued down the centuries and other inspired writings included, instead of the canon being closed, then the modern " Bible " might well include some fragments of Browning such as this :—

[1] Job 19[25]. [2] Job, 42[2].
[3] Rom. 8[28]. [4] 2 Tim. 1[12].

Sorrow is hard to bear, and doubt is slow to clear,
Each sufferer says his say, his scheme of the weal and
    the woe :
But God has a few of us whom He whispers in the
    ear ;
The rest may reason and welcome : 'tis we musicians
    know.

But do these enheartening declarations deserve the word " know "? What *is* knowledge ?

I think we must define knowledge as the greatest degree of probability. We cannot say more than this, because what we call " knowledge " is modified and re-modified as new facts come into view, and omni-science would be necessary to know all, and deity to know anything completely. " How little we know ! " is the cry of the greatest scientists, philosophers and theologians. All say with St. Paul, " We know in part." [1]

As I see it, there are two roads towards knowledge.

(1) One is intellectual and is called science.

(2) The other is intuitive and is called faith.

The first is not our province just now, but

[1] I Corin. 13⁹.

I would like to make three comments on it, because it so often gives itself airs, as though it were the only way of reaching certainty.

(a) Scientific knowledge is temporary in all its conclusions. The astronomical conclusions of a hundred years ago were far different from those of today. Yet they were claimed as knowledge. Jeans's conclusions in the astonomical field would have been incredible and fantastic to the astronomer of a century ago. The same is true of any field of enquiry. So what is " proved " by science turns out to be a temporary hypothesis, and what is " known " turns out to be the most likely explanation of phenomena which can be reached at any particular time. So many things have happened that scientists declared impossible. For instance, a scientist attacked Stephenson when he made his first engine and *proved* that no human body could move at so high a speed as forty miles per hour and live! So when science says she " knows ", we need a pinch of scepticism. She really means she " believes ". And that is a word of faith.

(b) The " knowledge " of science is itself
more the product of faith than we com-
monly suppose : faith in the reliability of the
mind's method of making deduction, faith in
the supposed uniformity (of the laws discovered) throughout the universe. Indeed,
what a queer saying it is that the exception
proves the rule. It tests the rule. It *dis-
proves* the uniformity of the rule, and one
wonders how many unknown exceptions
there are to every known rule. Indeed,
to say that 2 and 2 equal 4 is a venture of
faith, for the working of the mind may be
illusory. To assert your own existence is a
statement of faith, and some philosophers
could be found who would say that that,
too, is illusion. Everything said to be
" known " can be dethroned by the sceptic
who challenges the reliability of the mind's
way of so reaching conclusions through
deductive reasoning. We *believe* we are
not being deceived by our mental processes,
so we arrive at conclusions which we claim
represent the highest degree of probability.
Of these conclusions we say we " know ",
but faith is required at every stage of every
argument.

(*c*) Faith has been the road to scientific knowledge in every branch of science. Haeckel, the biologist, said, "Scientific *faith* fills the gaps in our knowledge of natural laws with temporary hypotheses." Scientists have made the glorious guess, the leap of faith, and then tested the guess and found evidence for it.

. . . . .

But turn to the second road to knowing. It is intuitive, but I hold that it is just as reliable a way of reaching truth as the other. It is reached when its alternative is rejected by some high court of assessment within the breast.

Take some most obvious illustrations : That a sunrise is beautiful, that the song of a bird pleases more than the wail of a siren warning us of an air raid, that parts of the Bible have greater value as literature than a penny dreadful, that St. Francis lived a noble life. . . . Scientific proof of these statements is not possible. But they cannot be denied without violating a court of judgment in the breast, whose authority is based on the ultimate values of human assessment.

I

I think some of the great affirmations
of religion are in this category. That
man lives after death, for instance, that
God can deal with sin, and so on. I am
not pleading for the way those affirmations
are worked out, but for their *basic* truth.
For their contradiction denies the sense
of rightness and meaningfulness at the core
of our being.

One type of sceptic will sneer at this and
call it wishful thinking. I cannot deny it,
but I see no ground for valid criticism in
the admission. That the war will end is
wishful thinking, but the statement is
not invalidated or untrue for that reason.
Religion's affirmations are not *merely* wishful
thinking. They have objective and prag-
matic support. That I should be saved
from sin is wishful thinking, but not dis-
credited on that account. The same is
true of a wish to survive death. The
negative positions are more incredible than
the positives. For instance, that the
whole natural process should be consum-
mated in producing man and that then
every part of him should be blotted out
by a splinter of shell or an invasion of

germs is irrational. To wish a thing true doesn't prove a thing is true, but it doesn't prove it is not true. And if we can put mere self out of the matter and put God in, the wishful thinking of the higher self is surely an evidence of truth, for when you think truly of God you cannot wish better than the truth.

Another type of sceptic will turn up his nose at anything called faith. It is important to remind him that everybody walks by some kind of faith. To say there is no God, no meaning in life, no moral purpose, no age-long plan, no deliverance from sin, no life after death, is to make statements in faith, for none of them is scientifically proved.

" That man is the product of causes which had no prevision of the end they were achieving; that his origin, his growth, his hopes and fears, his loves and beliefs, are but the outcome of accidental collocations of atoms; that no fire, no heroism, no intensity of thought and feeling can preserve an individual life beyond the grave; that all the labours of the ages, all the devotion, all the inspiration, all the noonday brightness of human genius, are destined to extinction in the vast death of the solar system, and that the whole temple of Man's achievement must inevitably be buried beneath the debris of a universe in ruins—all these things, if not quite beyond dispute, are yet so nearly certain that no philosophy which rejects them can hope to stand. Only within the scaffolding of these truths, only on the firm foundation of unyielding despair, can the soul's habitation henceforth be safely built."

That is the faith of Bertrand Russell as expressed in his " Sceptical Essays ". Well, that is faith too ! There is certainly no proof of such a ghastly indictment.

But one feels entitled to let a poet make a comment on such a faith :—

> Let him walk in the gloom whoso will; peace be
>   with him, But whence is his right
> To declare that the world is in darkness, because he
>   has turned from the light,
> Or to seek to o'ershadow my day with the pall of
>   his self-chosen night? [1]

In these days I find that there are three

[1] Solomon Solis-Cohen.

great declarations which help me greatly. They are declarations of faith. I cannot prove them. But their denial is in conflict with what I have called the court of assessment in my heart. Their denial would ask more of belief than their affirmation. Jesus believed them, and He—to put it at its lowest—was a religious Expert. I should hesitate to oppose Dr. Jeans on a matter of astronomy or Professor Bragg on a matter of physics, much more Jesus on a matter of religious belief.

The first is that God reigns, the second that God cares, the third that God strives.

The first declares that " the Lord God Omnipotent reigneth ", that no evil can overthrow His throne, that the world has not run amok and got out of control, that He is still in charge and His values are still supreme   Nothing can make beauty ugliness. Nothing can make truth lies. Nothing can make evil goodness. No evil force can reverse God's ultimate values.

The second declares that God has a plan for every life and will bring it to *His* goal at last. Every individual is of infinite importance to Him, and, this side of the

grave or the other, He will bring that life
to its true destiny.

The third declares that God is ever striving, not just remotely watching. Hindered
here, turned by man's misuse of free will
from any speedy achievement of His will
there, going down with men into their
failure and disaster and suffering and pain,
He is endlessly striving in every way, save
coercion, to bring men into harmony with
His will, using even evil—as He used the
Cross—to achieve His mighty ends. His
omnipotence does not mean that everything that happens is His will. It means
that nothing that happens can defeat His
will. Even those who do evil will find that
it has been turned in the long run from
their ends to His.

Now let us apply some aspects of the
Christian faith to some very modern conditions. Let us subtract faith's triumphant
declarations and then add them and see
where we get.

Here is a man whose boy is missing or
killed in the war. Let us subtract faith.
I can say, " Well, it's hard luck. I'm very
sorry. It was a good cause [though I am

not sure to what extent it is " good " if
faith in God and goodness goes]. You
won't see him again, but you must try to
get over it. Wasted lives are very sad,
aren't they? . . ."

But now *add* faith. I can say, " May I
tell you what helped me most when I lost
one who was dear to me? You will miss
him horribly, but he's quite safe in God's
loving care. You will meet him again and
find that nothing is lost. God will use your
boy's sacrifice to further His august plans.
God gave His own Son in a mighty cause.
Try not to fret, or you may be lessening
your boy's happiness on the other side.
Hang on to your faith in God and you
yourself will be made a finer character
because of the fire you're passing through."

Here is a man who has fallen into despair
because of the woe and trouble in the world.
Subtract faith. Dwell on war and war's
effects in China and Japan and Spain and
Abyssinia, in Finland, in Norway and
Holland and Belgium and France and Greece
and Britain. Spread out the desolation and
sorrow and pain and the apparent futility of
war. Suicide seems the most rational

activity. Let us escape into nothingness from this intolerable meaninglessness !

Then add faith ! Show a man that the very extent of evil shows the power of a God who dare let such horror be so widespread, without just wiping humanity off the slate and starting afresh, knowing He can still redeem His world without loss, and use its evil for His purposes. Speak of the challenge it all makes to his own faith in God, that God cannot lose, cannot be defeated; that others are watching his reactions and can be made brave by his courage. The man with faith added may go out a finer character in this evil world than he was when all was ease and comfort and luxury.

" My son has been grievously hurt in an air raid," says a man, " and the doctor thinks he may suffer for the rest of his life." Subtract faith in God and what a desolate situation ! Would you not rather be able to speak of what a fine character can do with suffering, making it a focus point of spiritual power ? Would you not rather be able to say that not what happens to us but our reaction to what happens to us is of supreme importance? That there is no suffering that cannot be caught up into God's plans, united with the suffering of Calvary and used in the redemption of the world?

There is no situation before which the Christian religion breaks down and confesses itself unable to do or say anything about it. I know of no other philosophy of life about which that can be said. In a sense these dark days are great days for religion. All days of calamity are.

What other philosophy of life has a relevant word to speak on big things and little things, pleasant things and unpleasant things, wealth and poverty, suffering and health, life and death? I know none. But the view of God and His relation to the world which Christ opened up to us takes in wars and the welfare of babies, earthquakes and ants, flaming nebulæ in the heavens and the microbes that infest a wound, the soaring mind of a saint and the foul practices of a concentration camp. There is nothing concerning which Christianity cannot say some relevant, illuminating and strengthening word.

Throughout His vast universe this royal

God reigns, and in every part He strives, caring for us all, the good and the bad, bearing our sorrows, hindered by our sins, wounded in all our pain, but ever marching on, in calamity as in the years of peace and ease, towards His triumph. Have faith in God! Lift up your fear-stricken hearts to Him. Lift up your tear-filled eyes to Him! Rest your harassed, wounded spirit on Him! Step out bravely because you find new strength in Him! And believe that He is giving to you NOW all you need to face life quietly, bravely, triumphantly, victoriously. "For this is the victory that overcometh, even our faith."

CHAPTER SEVEN

FAITH'S SUPREME CLAIM

THOSE WHO HAVE FOLLOWED THE ARGU-
ment of this book so far will realise that we
have been in quest of a philosophy of life,
a way of looking at life which strengthens
the heart and mind to meet the problems
of these days. In the chapter called
" Faith's Triumphant Declarations " we
mentioned three great affirmations about
God which seem particularly relevant to
our troubled lives today : (i) God rules,
(ii) God cares, (iii) God strives; and our
conclusion was that if these tremendous
propositions about God were really believed, then the soul could stand up to
almost any distress that was poured upon
it. The body might break down in the
strain and the nervous system collapse.
This does not argue any breakdown of
faith. And the truth about God can keep
faith triumphant in a falling world, even

if physically and nervously and psychologically we may not be able to stand the intense strain of war.

But faith goes farther, and makes a supreme claim, the claim that we may " know " not merely facts about God, but know God Himself. This is the very heart of religion. The most important thing is not that we should believe certain propositions about God, although that is vital and can do a great deal to steady us. The supremely important thing is to *believe in God*. Not merely to rest the mind by recalling those things that He is doing, or certain statements that have been made about Him, but to know Him for Himself, to love Him, to trust Him, to worship and adore Him as our unfailing Friend, our unerring Guide, our adequate, omnipotent God.

I think I can illustrate that by a few very simple pictures. Let us imagine that a boy has left home to make his way in the world. He has gone to the University, let us say, or to some business, and let us imagine that he gets into some kind of trouble or scrape. Make a mental picture of this youth sitting down in his room and saying to himself, " I wonder what my father would advise me to do? " Then let us imagine him writing to his father, receiving in due course a reply full of tender advice, and also, perhaps, a cheque to pay the police-court fine ! But what a difference in that situation if the father suddenly walked into the boy's room ! Can't you imagine that boy rising up and saying, " Why, dad, this is grand ! I was just longing for you " ? Certain things that his father had done or promised to do for him had already comforted him. Certain things that his father had taught him had already meant something to him. Certain assurances from his father had strengthened his mind and heart. But what a difference when his father *came* ! That is what makes a person, receiving bad news of a loved one, rise up and say, " I must go to him." We must not only know the truth about God, what God has done, and the many true statements made about Him. We must know God—present, real, loving, and close to us in our troubles.

Here is another picture. Let us imagine

a little evacuee girl, separated from her mother. (And one can understand what some little children are going through just now. They won't show it very much, but some little children must be going through an agony of lonely fretting. It is quite against all the laws of God that a little child should be indefinitely separated from her own mother.) Let us imagine this little girl tossing on her bed, worried, tearful, deeply troubled about something. I wonder if you can imagine her head pressed into the pillow, trying to stop the tears, and saying to herself, " Now, what was it Mummy told me to say when I felt lonely ? What was it she told me to do if I could not sleep ? " She is comforting her mind and heart by something that is true about her mother, by some words her mother told her to say. But supposing her mother walked into the room and sat on her bed. The little girl would not need to believe propositions or recall words written down or spoken long ago. She would enter into immediate communion with a loving person, and that is more important still. I want to get you, if you will, to pass on from all the things which in the last four or five chapters on this matter I have written *about* God. If this book is really going to help you, it ought to go on from persuading you to accept certain propositions concerning God to persuading you to know God for Himself, a Person present, here and now, who can be trusted and who says, " I will never leave you nor forsake you."

So, if distress and suffering do come upon us, or if they have come upon us, we shall find tremendous help from our Bible, and enormous comfort and strength from thinking about those great truths concerning God, which are part of our faith; but we shall find the greatest sense of peace and happiness, if we can pass from believing to trusting, from believing things about Him, into real, direct communion with Him.

If I had a voice that would reach the whole nation I would call it, and recall it, to that great truth; but I don't need to, because it has been done by one better equipped and with greater authority. " God is the best Friend with whom a man can share life or death." That is a quotation which sounds like an Archbishop, but it is our Foreign Secretary making a reply to Hitler. Those words come from one of his recent broadcast speeches. I have never lifted up my heart to God with greater thankfulness than I did to think that a Foreign Secretary of this country should call people to prayer, and talk like this to the nation. Can you conceive a greater difference ? On the one hand Hitler's hysterical outcry, his blatantly expressed ambition to add the British Empire to his bag of enslaved nations; on the other hand this calm sense of complete security and assurance in God, a search for God's will and a prayer for courage to do it whatever the cost. So let me add my little emphasis to that authoritative word of Lord Halifax.

. . . . .

To me one of the most important words in any of the creeds is the word " in ". " I believe *in* God the Father, Almighty, Maker of Heaven and Earth. . . ." Some credal phrases are not, to me, very important. " Born of the Virgin Mary " is not very important in my view. I depend on what He said and was and did in the world, not on how he came into it. " He descended into Hell." That is not to me a matter of vital significance. I am not a bit clear as to what it means. What is much more important than believing things about a person is believing in a person. As you believe in a person, the things that you believe *about* a person become less and less significant, less and less important. Is not that true in regard to our human friendships ? If you have a real friend and you are in conversation with somebody else about that friend, and that somebody else begins to disparage your friend, you say, " Wait a minute, I *know* him." If they persist and offer more arguments, you say, " I am certain he could explain it if he were here." You have got past the point when things that are said *about* a person matter, because you know the person, and have been in communion with the person. Your trust *in* him is bigger than your *belief* about him.

I am certain that we have got to get there in regard to God. After all, the things that we might be told about God

K

might damage our faith, if our faith is only believing things concerning Him. The clever sceptic does make up a very damning indictment against God, as some evil-disposed person could make up a damning indictment against a great surgeon, by taking his little boy of five on one side and telling the tale from a particular angle. That person could say, " Do you know that your father gets a person unconscious on a table, and when he is insensible and can't defend himself, your father cuts his body with a sharp knife and takes part of it away. How would you like to have that done to you ? " But you can't break a child's faith in his father thus if that father is a real friend to his small son. If the child could argue, he would say, " I *know* my Daddy. I will leave all you have said for further light."

In a similar way you could make up an indictment against God. " I don't think much of a God who allows all this evil in the world. Why didn't He save my friend from death ? Why doesn't He *do* something ? Why does He allow war to spoil His lovely world and bring suffering to thousands?" But the person who has *known* God, and not merely known about God, says, "Well, I can't understand yet. I have got to leave many things unexplained. But I know God." One is reminded of that great word of St. Ignatius, "He who hath heard the Word of God can bear His silences."

As I was writing this very chapter, I received a letter from a nurse in one of the London Hospitals who says: "A small child came in for an operation. As I went to take him from the arms of his father, he gave truly heart-rending sobs. 'Don't let them, Daddy', he cried. 'Don't let them take me?' I chanced to glance at the father's face, and I have never forgotten the agony I saw. It was indescribable. Yet for the sake of the child, he allowed me to take him without a word and turned hurriedly away. Yet how could a small child understand his father's purpose?"

It often seems to us that God allows His children to be tortured in ways that are meaningless. It is only because we are too small to understand. If only we could see the agony in His own face we could understand better. In the face that looked down from the Cross we can. Yet those tortured lips still called God, " Father ". When we hear the Word of God, we can bear His silences and await His explanations.

We are not to stop at believing propositions about God ; we are to trust God, and I want to ask you to do that. Get to know God ! Our faith is weak so often because we believe propositions about God, some of which we have made up ourselves. We have said, " Well, if He is God, He ought to do this and that." Wait a minute ! Can this little mind of man understand what He is doing, any more than a child of five can understand surgery and anæsthesia ? And while there are ever so many propositions that are going to help man, there are going to be damning statements about God that the enemy can make. My faith will crash unless it has got past believing things about Him, to believing in Him. You can say, " I trust that if God is God, this will happen and that will happen." But if you believe in Him you will say, " I shall trust Him whatever happens." Only that can hold you steady.

We are so concerned to get propositions about God right instead of getting our relationship with God right. Understanding is much less challenging, but much less important. Doesn't *faith* in Christ really mean believing in God on Christ's responsibility without demanding to be made to understand first ?

Religion, which is intellectually difficult, is actually simple. It is intellectually very difficult. I mean that if religion could only spread as men's minds were intellectually satisfied, we should fail with some of the best people. On the one hand are the people who are so simple that you could not possibly win faith for them and in them by trying to prove propositions to them. On the other hand are people who have had such a lot of intellectual training that it makes them incapable of accepting certain statements. Some people are so simple they cannot grasp things, and others so idolatrous in regard to scientific proof that they cannot accept things. We shall fail with both if we are limited to proving things about God. The point is that the best faith can be grasped by the simple people and by the most intellectual. It passes from knowing things about God to faith in a Person, and trust in Him and love for Him.

I wonder if you know this poem of Walter C. Smith. It is really a picture of a man who, in earlier days, was appalled by the findings of " modernism ". He felt that when the higher critics took the Old Testament to pieces, his whole faith was threatened. He was foolishly trying to hold a line from Genesis to Revelation, and could not bear to think that any point in that long line of defence was weak. Hear how he regained perspective and true faith :—

> They dried up all my Jacob's wells,
>   They broke the faithful shepherd's rod,
> They blurred the gracious miracles,
>   Which are the signature of God.
>
> In trouble then and fear I sought
>   The Man who taught in Galilee,
> And peace unto my soul was brought
>   And all my faith came back to me.
>
> O times of weak and wavering faith
>   That labour pleas in His defence,
> You only dim Him with your breath,
>   He is His own best evidence.

Jesus, you perceive, very rarely offered men's hearts arguments about God. He

did sometimes, but that was not His usual
way. Sometimes I wonder why, and I
think it is because people's minds can't
take away an argument about God. I
have erred in this by presenting arguments
about God to those to whom I preach.
But if they and I could meet in the years
ahead, and I said, " How many sermons of
mine can you remember? " I don't think
they would be able to produce arguments.
They would remember the illustrations.
" I remember when you told the story
about so and so," they would say. Jesus
knew the workings of the mind, and He
told parables that were stories about a
Person who was lovable and to be trusted.
You can put your intellectual equipment
on one side. In many a problem we
simply have to put our intellectual equipment on one side. It is not good enough
to confirm our faith. It goes a little
way and then breaks down. We will try
to " justify the ways of God to men ".
We try to save God from being misunder-
stood or thought unkind. We argue His
case with desperate enthusiasm. This is
not to be criticised as long as we realise

that in many problems the human mind just cannot deliver God from the charges of the sceptic. We don't know enough and can't see far enough. But faith in a living, loving Person whom we know in our experience can leap in when argument breaks down.

The Master was content to paint pictures of God and leave some things without explanation. There must have been many times when He could do no more than that without bewildering His hearers' minds.

We make many mistakes in our preaching by not remembering that. So often when a " great preacher " preaches to a congregation, people go home and say, " No doubt he is a great man and very clever, but it was all over my head." But the words of Jesus were so profound that people have been discussing them for two thousand years, and now they have not plumbed those depths of meaning. Yet " the common people heard Him gladly ". They said, in effect, " It was marvellous. He made life look so different. He made God so lovable." God was seen to be a Person you could trust and turn to in your sorrow and pain. When He was hanging on the Cross, Jesus did not say, "Father, I thank Thee that now my intellect understands and everything is explained." Would you be shocked if I said it was part of His humanity that He could not have said that? He did not say, "Now I understand everything." He said, "Father, into Thy hands I *trust* my spirit." That is the final word of faith. Trust based on a personal relationship with One, who may be a multitude of things we shall never understand, but who is utterly dependable, final power and everlasting love.

Look just at this picture from life! Here are two men in deep trouble. One goes into a study and pulls down volume after volume and thrashes out argument after argument, and writes down some great declarations about God. And I am not going to disparage that: it is of tremendous value. But I know a man who, when he was in deep trouble, went into a wood and was quiet and opened his heart to God, and amid the singing of the birds, the music of the wind, and the loveliness of the trees, God Himself came. This man could not have argued very much, could not have mastered abstruse intellectual propositions, or thought his way through the theories of the theologians. But he came out of that wood with his eyes shining and his heart at rest and a song in his spirit, because ten minutes of communion with God can take us further than ten years study *about* Him. That is what is offered. That is the heart of the matter. That is faith's supreme claim. That is faith's holy of holies. When you get there, then whatever is said about Him, you will be able to say, " I know Him, I have met Him, I have communed with Him; and whatever He may do, I shall never lose trust in Him. Whatever happens to me doesn't matter, it won't break my belief in Him."

Do you remember those words of St. Paul? [1] " For I know whom I have believed, and am persuaded that He is able to keep that which I have committed unto Him against that day." Is the order of the sentence accidental? I don't think so. " I know *whom*," and then, " I am persuaded " about all those other things concerning

[1] 2 Tim. 1[12].

Him. As you know Him, that is what
happens. There is a victory for us there,
through faith, which can never know defeat.
" This is the victory that overcometh, even
our faith."

CHAPTER EIGHT

FAITH'S FINAL SECURITY

WHEN ALMOST ALL THINGS SEEM INSECURE it is important that the Christian should be able to answer the question, Where, if anywhere, can ultimate security be found? The cry " Safety first " may be unworthy, but the cry for security is natural enough. It was Jesus who praised the man who, setting out on a venture, sat down first to count the cost.[1] And if even the *soul* knows no ultimate harbour from which it cannot be driven by whatever storms may arise, if, in the adventure of life, there is no ultimate security, if all may be taken from us, if everything can be lost in the wreck, then it is a question whether life is worth living, whether the gift of life is justifiable, whether we are not thrust back into meaninglessness once more.

If I embarked on some business venture,

---

[1] Luke 14[28].

one of the words I am sure my bank manager would use is the word " security ". The good business mind will take risks to win a fortune, but there is a natural craving for some kind of security.

With what immense relief some of us have heard the medical specialist declare that our dear one is out of danger ! She may have much yet to suffer, but we have been given a sense of security that she will come through. All is not lost. Though still suffering we feel she is safe.

Every psychologist, and most ministers, know how poignantly the soul of man cries out to have that ultimate sense of safety. Many of our hymns voice this longing,

> Jesu, Lover of my soul
> Let me to Thy bosom fly. . . .
> Safe into the haven guide,
> O receive my soul at last.

The longing to feel safe !

Sometimes it isn't a very healthy longing, and religion has got into bad odour with the psychologists for being escapist. Real Christianity isn't escapist, for it has sent more men and women out voluntarily into heroic and costly adventure than any other philosophy of life.   But unfortunately many perversions of Christianity exist, and he who tries to take the comfort and will not accept the challenge has made out of Christian material a neurosis, a faulty adaptation of himself to life and of life to himself.   Such a cave may be useful to hide in for a time but it is not the Christian Faith and it may crash in on him when he needs it most.

We must not stay here to attempt to deal adequately with those alluring and false ways by which Christ's message has been perverted to comfort the frightened and make His religion a deep and cushioned dug-out for timid souls to hide in when the going above ground is particularly arduous, though that is a task which cries out to be done.

Yet there is a legitimate sense in which the soul cries out for security. ' Are there any conditions,' men ask, ' which one may fulfil so that one can win that delicious sense of safety *whatever happens* ? '

I am sure there are.   In this chapter I should like to try to show what the answer to that question is, then to show how the mind, from infancy to senility, is seeking out that security, then to show how Christ Himself sought security and found it, and how the saints seem to say to us that from the storms of life we may find temporary shelter here, and then there, and then elsewhere, but that from a to z there is only one harbour from which the soul can never be driven, and in a phrase it is by *possessing God Himself and the truth concerning Him.*

Let us examine this more closely. One of the reasons why so many people find that religion appears to let them down is that what they call faith is assent instead of belief.

I do not find it easy exactly to express this difference, but it is as profound as is possible. There is all the difference in the world between the truth to which the intellect says " yes " and which the emotions accept with easy acquiescence, on the one hand, and, on the other hand, the truth which takes hold of both mind and heart in a captivity that alters the reactions of the entire personality. Perhaps one might say it is the difference between troops passing through a country and troops seizing a country, taking charge of its internal economies, managing its railways, its food distribution, its banks and transport. Perhaps one might say it is the difference between the sound of the band to the soldier and—if it is not an anachronism —the sword in the hand of the soldier. The music invigorates, cheers, inspires. Heads go up, shoulders back, feet lifted. So acts on the spirit even the truth to which mere assent is given. But in battle, the music of the band soon dies away. Woe to him who in battle depended on the band! On the other hand the sword has been acquired, but it has become part of the soldier. He can *use it*. He cuts his way through opposing forces with it. It means most in the hour of greatest need. So is the truth which the mind possesses; the truth which possesses the mind.

There is one revealing verse in the Fourth Gospel which puts the matter in a nutshell. The men of Samaria said to the woman, " Now we believe, not because of thy much speaking (that brought assent), but we have heard *for ourselves* and *know* that this is indeed the Saviour of the world " (that is true belief).

In our psychological clinic we sometimes

have a patient whose trouble is traced back
to what we call "conscience distress".
Some sin, perhaps of the long ago, has never
really been adequately dealt with or even
faced, and it festers there, perhaps in the
unconscious, a cause of distress to mind,
and even body.   Having brought the hidden
thing to light, the grand treatment is to offer,
in Christ's name, the forgiveness of sins.
But it is one thing to *offer* forgiveness, and
another thing to get it accepted.   "God
will forgive you," we say, "He is offering
forgiveness here and now."   The patient
frequently replies, "Yes, I know."   But
does he?   He assents.   He knows there is
a Christian doctrine of forgiveness taught in
churches and widely accepted.   He would
advance no arguments against such a
doctrine.   On the contrary, he most de-
voutly wants to "believe" it.   But it
isn't easy for him or for us.   When he
believes, when he gets the truth right into
his ductless glands, as it were, when the
glorious truth flashes into his very soul, I
have known the facial expression alter and
bodily health improve.   At last he *possesses*
the truth and is possessed by it.   But so

L

often the great truths of God are what June
was to the captive in William Watson's
poem " Estrangement "—" a legend emptied
of concern " :

Thus may a captive in some fortress grim,
From casual speech betwixt his warders, learn
That June on her triumphant progress goes,
Through arched and bannered woodlands; while for
    him
She is a legend emptied of concern,
And idle is the rumour of the rose.

I say to one man, " Bereavement is sad,
isn't it ? " Perhaps such a man has never
had a sad moment in his life. I can win his
assent. But let me say the same thing to
one who has just looked for the last time on
the face of his beloved dead, and, with a
look in his eyes searching and steadfast, he
may make the same answer. But what a
world between ! One assents. The other
believes and knows and realises with all his
being.

I may have laboured the point overmuch.
But the most important thing in the world
is to know God for oneself, to be sure of Him,
to be able to rely on the truths about Him,
not because one has sung hymns and heard
sermons and read books, but because one

has proved truth in experience. Only there is security found, only there can the spirit rest without any fear at all that anything in earth or heaven or hell can tear one from that blessed anchorage.

. . . . .

Now watch man's mind, from infancy onward, feeling for safety.

The newly born child, it is said, only brings with him into the world two fears : the fear of being dropped and the fear of a loud noise. For nine happy months he has been safely carried and swung, and he has heard nothing but the beating of his mother's heart and the pulsing of her arteries.[1] As soon as he is born, the child claims from those who surround him the sense of safety.

But very soon the quest for physical safety seems to express itself more rarely. A kind of spiritual security is sought.   The

[1] These factors possibly explain our love of rhythm and also the methods the harassed parent adopts at two in the morning to get a baby to sleep, keeping him warm, rocking him, crooning to him and thus supplying the next-best-thing to the pre-natal conditions in which the child was happy and which he has recently left.

child seems to put down anchors, he estab-
lishes a sense of values, and his trust in
those who appear to personify them is his
way of feeling secure.

Let me illustrate this. A little girl of
eight was brought to our psychological clinic
by her mother, who complained that the
child suffered from night-terrors and other
nervous symptoms which had all developed
since a certain date. The child, said the
mother, cried out in her sleep in a state of
apparent anguish. When asked what the
child said, the mother demurred for a little,
and then replied, " The words she cries out
are, ' He didn't really do it, did he,
mummy ? ' "

To make a long story short, the father
was in prison. The symptoms developed
in the child from the day she found that out.
She had sought in vain to " explain " her
father's absence to her schoolmates. They
had twitted her with his crimes. It was no
good appealing to her mother, for she had
" put the child off " with a story of her
father having had to go away on business.
On the day the child found out about her
father's character, the anchor-chain which

held her little character safely and gave it
security snapped, and she drifted like a
helpless ship at sea.

One would like to try to convince all
parents, and parents to be, that God's plan
is not only that every child should have the
loving care of a father and mother, but also
the spiritual anchorage which the characters
of a *good* father and a *good* mother, with
sympathy and understanding, provide.

Fortunately, God does not leave the child
alone. In a strange way there comes to
most children, even to the child comparatively uninstructed about religion, a mysterious sense of companionship with a beneficent
Friend who stands by to help and sympa-
thise. I must not write at length on this,
or this chapter will become another book.
The idea is beautifully worked out in Mr.
Hugh Walpole's novel, " The Golden Scare-
crow ".

The psychologist realises something of
what happens in a child's mind when, in
the hour of anguish, he turns to his cherished
possessions—a doll, a " Teddy ", an old,
stuffed horse. Longing for comfort and
security, and finding it neither in man nor

God, he turns to his toys. The law of the association of ideas has made him realise that the happiness associated with an object in an hour of joy may sometimes be recovered by turning to the same object in hours of sorrow.

This is the inwardness of one of the most lovely and tender poems in our language, Coventry Patmore's, " The Toys ".

My little son, who look'd from thoughtful eyes,
And moved and spoke in quiet grown-up wise,
Having my law the seventh time disobey'd,
I struck him, and dismiss'd
With hard words and unkiss'd,
—His Mother, who was patient, being dead.
Then, fearing lest his grief should hinder sleep,
I visited his bed,
But found him slumbering deep,
With darken'd eyelids, and their lashes yet
From his late sobbing wet.
And I, with moan,
Kissing away his tears, left others of my own;
For, on a table drawn beside his head,
He had put, within his reach,
A box of counters and a red-veined stone,
A piece of glass abraded by the beach,
And six or seven shells,
A bottle with bluebells,
And two French copper coins, ranged there with careful art,
To comfort his sad heart.

Pathetic and tender in the child ! But how sad it is to see a grown man or woman clutching at " things " as the only known security. There are storms about just now which can sweep all that away in a night. Woe unto him who has his security only in his possessions, or even in his own life ! For such securities may be stripped from him, and his own life is only his last material possession.

We notice next how the mind finds anchorage in friendship. The schoolboy admires a master who is a Rugger " blue ". The girl adores Miss Jones, writes to her, imitates her ways, and waits all day for one smile from the goddess for whom she has a " pash ".[1]

The objects of such adoration should not be unduly elated. It is not they, but the qualities they are supposed to possess, which provide the child's security. Unconsciously to the child, his mind is putting down its anchor in rock-values which it admires. As those values change, Miss Jones will pass into a blessed oblivion. These values are only the temporary harbours of the soul.

[1] *La grande passion.*

But they are in the plan of God. What
a lot friendship means to us in these difficult
days ! The most glorious thing in marriage
is surely to have a friendship which is like
a quiet haven into which the ship of life,
tossed all day in storms and cross currents,
may creep in and find rest and peace.
Husband should be able to offer that
anchorage to wife, and wife to husband.
Blessed are they who have at least one
friend to whom to go and find a sure and
peaceful retreat.

One could go on. Some souls turn to
Nature or great music, to great poetry, to
great art, and find anchorage there. . . .

It seems to me as though God says to us,
from the cradle to the grave, " You want
to feel safe, you need the feeling of security,
an anchorage, a haven. Very well, you
can *for a time* find it here and there, in a
parent's strong character and unfailing
love, in your possessions, in your friendships, in whispers of God to be heard in
the deep woods, in mighty mountains, in
the laughing meadows and the chattering
streams, in poetry, music and art, in wife
or husband ; but all these are temporary.

They are not the final harbour. There
is only one Anchorage from which no
tempest can drag you, one Harbour from
which no storm can drive you, and that is
to possess and be possessed by Me." He is
the one " Shelter from the stormy blast
and our eternal Home." Not a Shelter,
indeed, for the body or nerves or mind, but
certainly for the spirit. We are not to fear
them that kill the body, and after that
have no more that they can do.[1] The soul
God will guard and keep inviolate. In this
sense He is a Refuge and Strength, a very
present help in trouble.[2]

Let us see how Christ's own life illustrates
this. His babyhood surely was given the
security of His mother's arms and His
mother's love. His boyhood surely was
safeguarded by the strong, fine character of
Joseph. The first two words of the Lord's
Prayer are Joseph's everlasting memorial.
No one for whom the word " father " was
spoilt in childhood could have taught the
Fatherhood of God as Jesus did. But in
His young manhood, misunderstanding and
unhappiness must often have made Him

[1] Luke 12[4].   [2] Psalm 46[1].

lonely. His brothers nagged Him for perversely leaving the business to them and becoming a wandering preacher. It is not clear who spoke the words, " He is beside Himself ",[1] but it seems to have represented the family opinion.

Jesus found refuge in human friendship. What a wealth of insight into the needs of human nature we find in the words, " He chose Twelve *that they might be with Him* ", for His sake as well as theirs, because every great soul knows the horrible, desolating loneliness of greatness and longs for human comfort and the refuge of another's love. Yet when He needed them most, they " all forsook Him and fled ". There is a spiritual geography as well as a physical, and when He, the most daring of all Pioneering Adventurers, penetrated into the lonely wastes of human experiences, He went alone. No foot followed Him there. Perhaps no foot could. No imagination can even picture what He saw and felt and suffered. All security was torn from Him— save one—that He was God's Son, doing

[1] Mark 3[21].

God's will, for God's sake, and that God was with Him to the last.

Some have written that He felt deserted, even by God, on the Cross when He uttered that awful cry, " My God, my God, why hast Thou forsaken Me? " Only so, say some writers, can Christ know the worst that human hearts can experience.

It may be so. We can only stand afar off and wonder. But in my heart I don't believe that there is any experience from which God deliberately withdraws Himself. We may not be able to perceive His Presence, and it may certainly be that bodily or mental anguish can so crowd consciousness that the mind has no room for any other thought. But I cannot think that when He who had done nothing but His Father's will was so sore beset, when every other friend had let Him down, when His consciousness was not so crowded that He could not find room for a dying thief, that the Compassionate Father averted His face from His dearly-loved Son.

We do realise that when the mind is in anguish it often turns back to those things

which have given it comfort before. Every
Jewish boy knew the Psalter by heart in the
original. What is more likely than that in
His hour of agony the Master's mind went
back to the 22nd Psalm which begins :
" Eloi, Eloi, lama sabacthani "? but which
also contains passionate affirmations that
although man is deserted by all, his God will
never let the soul which believes on Him
perish in the dark.[1]

All through His life, as I read the Gospels,
beyond and above all temporary security,
the Master knew that strong bond, that
anchor-chain, that final and blessed security
of His Father's love. Of it He might surely
have said, in the words of the Latin tag,
teneo et teneor. He held fast to it and
was held fast by it. And it never let Him
go.

That final security is available for us.
All else can be torn from us. Parents misunderstand children. Children become impatient of efforts at parental discipline and

[1] Cf. verse 24 : " He hath not despised nor abhorred
the affliction of the afflicted. Neither hath He hid
His face from him. But when he cried unto Him,
He heard."

advice, and launch away on their own, feeling that the old folk " don't understand ".
The heroes and heroines of our schooldays
are found out to be quite ordinary folk.
Our idols have feet of clay. Even friendships are severed. Men and women drift
apart. Divorce courts are busy. Our possessions seem to count for very little when
our hearts are broken. In any case, a
bomb may take them all from us any night
between dusk and dawn. Hundreds of years
B.C. a sorrowful heart cried out, " Where
shall wisdom be found and where is the
place of understanding ? . . . The sea saith,
' It is not with me '." [1]   We love the mountains, the quiet lakes that mirror the sky,
the mysterious whisper of trees at dusk,
the gaiety of buttercups in the sunshine,
the holy hush of dawn, the majesty of the
starlit sky; but everyone who has mourned
has found that you have to be in the right
mood to receive their healing ministries,
and even when you do, it is largely because
you make them the media of a comfort that
comes from deeper sources than themselves.
Have those who dwell where Nature is

[1] Job. 28^{12-14}.

loveliest found no need of God? No missionary will give you any evidence for that conclusion. Music, art and literature, all are God's garment, but somehow there are hours when they will not speak to us unless we can find some faith in Him from somewhere, so that, touching the hem of His garment, the healing grace flows out to meet our bitter need.

No! This lowly, exalted thing called the human heart can feel safe only in God, and that not in any conventional, shallow thought of Him, but rather only when, by communion with Him, the soul can truly and sincerely say,

> I lift my heart to Thee,
> Saviour Divine;
> *For Thou art all to me,*
> And I am Thine.
> Is there on earth, a closer bond than this :
> That my Beloved's mine, and I am His? [1]

Then comes the delicious sense of well-being which the New Testament calls blessedness, when, even though it is rare for us to rise to such heights, we do in our

[1] C. E. Mudie.

deepest being know that nothing matters but God and our relationship with Him, that no calamity that can happen to us can spoil that relationship or take Him from us. We may lose our possessions, our friends, our dearest, our lives. We may be stripped of every protection, everything to which we cling, but nothing can take God from us, nor the sense that, possessing Him, and possessed by Him we " need have naught besides ". Nothing, nothing, nothing, can take us from His care, and in that blessed security the soul can rest. No storms blow here, and no winds come. No angry waves affright. Nothing can harm us any more.

> Home is the sailor, home from sea,
> And the hunter home from the hill.[1]

When we get into that rich experience of possessing God and being possessed by Him we can say about any so-called catastrophe what Rupert Brooke said about war :

> War knows no power. Safe shall be my going,
> Secretly armed against all death's endeavour ;
> Safe though all safety's lost ; safe where men fall ;
> And if these poor limbs die, safest of all.[2]

[1] R. L. Stevenson. " Requiem."
[2] Rupert Brooke. " Safety."

Yes, and we shall have won our little victory, and in our own small way be able to say with the Master, " I have overcome the world." " This is the victory that overcometh the world, even our faith."

PART II

SOME OF FAITH'S ALLIES

CHAPTER NINE

BEAUTY

I EXPECT MANY OF MY READERS WAKE UP in the morning and for ten seconds feel glad to be alive. The sunshine is streaming through the window and the birds are at matins. Then the mind is troubled by a sudden query—"What is wrong?" And in the tenth of a second comes the answer, "Oh, of course, the war!" And the old darkness falls upon the spirit for the rest of the day, until, if we are lucky, the nightly miracle of sleep wafts us away to a dreamland, where not even the horror of war follows us.

In writing thus I do not mean, of course, that the darkness of the spirit is unbroken. We have our routine work to do. Humour will keep breaking through. We try to keep bright. We hide our fears and depression. Yet, for most of us, just below the threshold of the mind's consciousness

lies a vast sea of anxiety; and a heavy
deluge of bad news, or, indeed, a message
that can all be written on a telegraph form,
is enough to raise the water-level and flood
our hearts and minds with distress.

We *must* find ways of escape. The mind
cannot be kept in good health if it is not at
times encouraged to breathe an ampler,
purer air. The mind kept constantly " on
the stretch " begins to lose its power of
resilience. War, to the imaginative, is one
long nightmare of horror. Let me urge
you to attempt at least a mental escape,
and support my plea by showing what
escape has meant to others. For temporary
escape to things that are of God makes
faith in Him more easy and gives the
mind a chance to regain its tone.

One day at Chequers a friend of Mr.
Stanley Baldwin—as he was then—reported his experiences in South-Eastern
Europe to the Prime Minister. The story
unfolded, and it was an ugly and depressing
one—plots and counter-plots, poverty and
oppression and vice. When the story was
finished a kind of silence of horror and
depression fell upon them both. Then Mr.

Baldwin pointed to a bowl of lovely roses on his table and said to his friend, " Plunge your face in those roses and thank God."

One is reminded of Tertullian's great saying, " If I give you a rose you won't doubt God any more." For indeed an offering of beauty to the grown man is quite different from the act of giving a pretty toy or a sweet to a child to distract him in a moment of childish grief. It is to present to the thoughtful mind an argument which runs roughly as follows : " The heart that planned what you call Beauty cannot be hostile or cruel or beastly, and your ability to appreciate and love beauty means that there is a kinship between you and the Reality which Beauty reveals. Rest your mind, then, not only in any form of Beauty which appeals to you, but in the truth that that Beauty represents, the abiding reality behind everything. Nothing can destroy Beauty or your apprehension of it. War and ugliness, horror and beastliness will pass. Beauty is one of the eternal values, and abides. Having rested in beauty for a time, you will go back with deeper dedication and greater energy and strength to combat evil. You will work the harder to make the world a place where all men can be happy and all things come into harmony with the Eternal Mind."

All beauty does this for us. Music, for instance.

A musician who by his singing had delighted Viscount Grey (then Sir Edward Grey, the Foreign Secretary) received a letter from him dated August 5th, 1914—the day after the Great War broke out—which included these sentences : " I love Handel's music, and it does me good. Europe is in the most terrible trouble it has ever known in civilised times, and no one can say what will be left at the end. But Handel's music will survive."

It may be the beauty of great literature to which you escape. Lady Oxford tells us in her Autobiography that just after the outbreak of war, in August 1914, she went one night into her husband's dressing-room and found him reading " Our Mutual Friend ". She writes, " He told me he was going to read all the Dickens novels, as they removed his thoughts, if only for a short time, from Colleagues and Allies."

Art has the same spell for some.

One of my friends, a lecturer in Biology at a famous university, even when he only went away from home for a night in order to lecture in another town, used to take with him a copy of some famous picture and set it up in an hotel bedroom and lie in bed and look at it, his body completely relaxed, because, he said, its beauty refreshed and renewed his spirit.

There is another aspect of beauty which I would recommend as mental escape from the depression war sets up. I mean the beauty of victorious living. I find in myself a new and keen love for great biographies. They give me back victorious faith.

We all long for ease and comfort, for release from the need for courage and sacrifice. If only life would leave us alone for a while, to eat and sleep in peace, to do our work and pursue our hobbies ! Yet the very thing that helps us most in great biography is the account of the way in which great men and women faced difficulty and hardship and refused to surrender to " the evil things " or the ugly things.

Even the memory of beauty can heal the

spirit. Canon Charles Raven, in his book, " In Praise of Birds ", wrote concerning the last war, " From the restless horror and hideousness of the war zone I could slip away to the imagined wonder of wave-washed rocks and the clamour of the seafowl and the eggs lying bare upon the ledges or bowered amid sea pink and campion."

So, if it is not too presumptuous, I would offer advice !

Before winter sets in or drags on another week, decide what forms of beauty make the most attractive appeal to you. It may be the loveliness of Nature, the dreaming moors, the mighty mountains, the mysterious woods. Your particular escape may be in the delight of studying birds, or flowers, or rocks, or insects.

It may be that you have never discovered the new world which music opens up, or art, or literature. I am told that anthologies of poetry are selling as they never sold before. What plans for a black-out winter open up for us ! To read Dickens or Scott through again. To read the life of Mozart, study and hear his music. To read a dozen books on birds and wander in

the country watching and identifying them
—particularly with some young friend.

But let me write a few lines of warning
about ways of escape. Those I have
mentioned are tonics, in my view, because
they take the mind back through Beauty
to the really lasting values. To take but
one example. The joy of witnessing a
grand sunset is surely that, though its glory
seems in a sense remote, there is something
within us that says, "I am somehow akin
to that." Our response to beauty is an
evidence that in some mystic, undefinable
sense we are one with it, one with Nature.
Our inherent greatness is stimulated by our
contact with the really great and lasting
things, like Beauty. So Beauty is a tonic
to us. We are more in love with life and
more ready to strive for the big things.

Some methods of escape are not. We
have all heard of the man who excused his
drunkenness to the Manchester magistrate
by saying, " It was the quickest way out
of Manchester." We have learned of the
" escape " which the betting fever produces
in terms of excitement, an excitement so
fierce that food and clothing have been

denied to little children and homes broken up and sold to provide the means of "escape". Such a means is not a tonic, but a drug. The palate is jaded, not delighted.

Perhaps a test lies just there as to whether a means of escape is a tonic or a drug. And "going to the pictures", good though that is, and often bringing to us some of the blessings of great art, can sometimes "let us down". For unless the things we see and hear have what Viscount Grey called "the eternal in them", I feel that we are uselessly trying to slake our thirst at broken cisterns. We may find distraction and recreation and enjoyment, and these are all worthy quests, but the thirst of the soul requires the eternal things which "the pictures" only seldom bring. Let me add, however, that some films bring one into contact with God more really than some church services.

Let me plead for a place for God. Prayer sounds to many a dull, stuffy thing. It is a tragedy that it is so, for watching birds or reading poetry can be a form of prayer. Prayer is communion with God—that, rather than merely asking for things. It is allowing oneself to be caught up into the life and purposes of God.

Prayer, of course, has many aspects, and our petitions for ourselves and intercessions for others are bound to take war into account. But I think prayer should contain the kind of thankful adoration which lifts the heart high above all world-worries and heart-cares to the serene, eternal life of God enthroned in that ultimate Beauty where truth and goodness are one.

It is the beauty and truth of thoughts about God on which the mind, in some quiet hour of prayer, can meditate, which bring the maximum tonic-sense of peace and rest, renewal and strength. Here is no mere anodyne; for the mind, so far from suffering the hangover effects of a drug, is made ready to grapple again with the grim ugliness of everyday life. Having pierced through to the Eternal Beauty—if only for a moment—we can face the ugliness with serenity, with confidence, with courage. For we know it is only of passing importance. It cannot destroy the real things. It only blots them from our sight for the moment.

We have seen a vision of the Eternal, and know it will come true.

So the Christ made escape again and again to the mountains, and then came back from the strengthening glimpse of the city of God's purpose to work in the foul slums of man's greed. He was transfigured on a high mountain, where again He breathed the air of that spiritual world where Moses and Elijah dwelt. Then He descended to cure an epileptic boy. He wept over men's sorrows, but not in sentimental escapism, for He died for their sins.

Religion that was mere escapism, making men run from reality into the dream-pictures of wishful thinking, would stand condemned and become itself the cause of neurosis. But religion that goes to God for men that it may go to men for God; that takes a look at the Eternal Beauty that it may be strengthened and inspired to bring that beauty to replace men's ugly ways; religion that draws the mind away to breathe the air of Heaven for awhile that it may face the fetid vapours of war and pain more bravely, determined with greater resolution to banish them from earth, is at once the soul's deepest need and greatest strengthening. By such a process faith recovers its perspective, restores its poise and balance, renews its health, returns to life with greater will to victory. And this is the victory that overcometh the world, even our faith.

CHAPTER TEN

HUMOUR

WHAT WITH WARS AND RUMOURS OF WARS over half the world, suffering and hardship for innumerable thousands and a general sense of insecurity which has a way—especially in the middle of the night—of undermining our serenity, we have some excuse for gloom.

For some the days are so solemn, so pregnant with foreboding that they will be impatient with me for writing about what seems to them so trivial a thing as humour. Someone is sure to write to me that I betray a shallow mind. " Here is the world falling to pieces about our ears," the writer will say, " and he devotes a chapter to an unimportant trifle like humour " !

In parenthesis, no one in these days should take irritable criticism too seriously. So many people are " nervy " and worked up. And when we get like that we have a habit of projecting our irritation on anything or anyone in our path. A man, criticised at work, comes home and takes it out of his wife, and then goes on to a church committee meeting and takes it out of the minister. Hitler has taken it out of us all, and unless we are careful and watchful we shall get irritable enough to take it out of innocent people and make their lives miserable.

My very parenthesis shows the need of humour, neither irreverent buffoonery like Voltaire's on the one hand nor cynical laughter like Swift's on the other, but all that is wholesome and healthy and integrating in " good humour "—the kind of humour which Macaulay said Addison possessed : " a mirth consistent with tender compassion for all that is frail, and with profound reverence for all that is sublime ". Humour is one of the best solvents in the world for the grit of irritation that gets into the cogs of life these days, and the man who can laugh at himself as well as at others will be among the last casualties in the war of nerves.

If this be true—and I hold that it is—

humour immediately appears to be a very
important thing indeed. It is a real tonic
of the soul and one of faith's finest allies.
Tennyson wrote, " I dare not tell you how
high I rate humour, which is generally most
fruitful in the highest and most solemn
human spirits. Dante is full of it. Shakespeare, Cervantes and almost all the greatest
have been pregnant with this glorious power.
You will even find it in the Gospel of Christ."

The Rev. J. Denholm Brash was a great
saint and the father of a friend of mine who
is a most lovable professor in a theological
college. When Denholm Brash died, there
lay on his bedside table a Bible and a copy of
Punch. I think we should be very wise if, in
these days of strain, we found our strength
in humour as well as solemn exhortation.

The soul needs, of course, those great,
solemn, enriching truths about God which
come to us from the Bible. But it does need
also—if it is going to " see life steadily and
see it whole "—those light touches which
give perspective, which maintain buoyancy,
which save us from taking anything, least of
all ourselves, too seriously.

Even death should come into that " any-

thing ". It was Donald Hankey, during
the last war, who wrote as follows : " Death
was in a way the greatest joke of all. In a
way, for if another fellow was hit, it was
an occasion for tenderness and grief. But
if one of them were hit—O death where is
thy sting? O grave where is thy victory?
Portentous, solemn Death you looked a fool
when you tackled one of them! Life?
They did not value life. They had never
been able to make much of a fist of it.
But if they lived amiss they died gloriously,
with a smile for the pain and the dread
of it. . . . With a gay heart they gave
their greatest gift, with a smile to think
that after all they had anything to give
that was of value. One by one death
challenged them. One by one they smiled
in his grim visage and refused to be dismayed. They had been lost; but they had
found the path that led them home; and
when at last they laid their lives at the feet
of the Good Shepherd, what could they do
but smile? " [1]

Some of us who lived and served with
those men know the place that humour

[1] Donald Hankey in *The Spectator*.

N

played in that grim struggle. Bairnsfather did something as well as the Bible. We knew the truth of a saying of R. M. Benson that " God gave us humour to save us from going mad." We understood the inwardness of that word of R. L. Stevenson, who, when he wrote it, had little cause for humour : " That people should laugh is a better preparation for life than many other things, higher and better sounding in the world's ear ". We could have underlined the brave words of Olive Schreiner that " the echoes of Despair slunk away, for the laugh of a brave, strong heart is death to them ".

We note how in great literature—Shakespeare, for instance—when minds have been made tense by some dramatic climax, they are relaxed by the introducing of some touch of humour. It must be so in everyday life. Your laughing has a place as well as your praying. There's a " time to weep and a time to laugh ", as the book of Ecclesiastes tells us.

Surely humour had a definite place in the ministry of Jesus. When sometimes I hear lessons read in church so solemnly, I see in imagination Peter and John in the back pew. They seem to nudge one another and say, " He wouldn't read like that if he had heard the Master talking." No one can really suppose that no ripple of laughter passed over the crowd, or that no humour was intended in His vivid picture of the fat old Pharisee drinking soup, straining out a gnat and swallowing a camel. Shut your eyes and imagine the camel going down !

" How many of us have ever pictured the process, and the series of sensations, as the long, hairy neck slid down the throat of the Pharisee—all that amplitude of loose-hung anatomy—the hump, two humps—both of them slid down, and he never noticed—and the legs—all of them—with the whole out-fit of knees and big-padded feet. The Pharisee swallowed a camel—and never noticed it." [1]

Here is another man fumbling to remove a speck from his brother's eye when a great plank sticks out of his own. Here is a man who lights a lamp and then puts it under the bed. Here is a picture of a man with his children in bed, a man who will not rise and

[1] T. R. Glover, " The Jesus of History."

give to his friend in the night for friendship's sake, but who, if the friend makes a noise enough, will rise and give him the whole house if only he won't wake the baby— the argument not being, of course, that God is reluctant to help us but will do so if we annoy Him by our continued prayers, but rather that if a mere man will, for a bad reason, consent to help one who is a nuisance, how much more will God, for a good reason, give to those who are His own children.

Who would believe that no laughter was intended, or that it did not break out, when Jesus told the story of the invitations to a feast which were evaded by one man who said he had bought a field and wanted to look at it, by another who had bought oxen and wanted to try them, and, most amusing of all, by a third who had married a wife who wouldn't let him go?

It is impossible to hold in the mind the thought of a perfect Man if we exclude all humour from His personality. Let us admit by all means the sorrowful side of His nature. For ever He is the Man of Sorrows and acquainted with grief. That side has been impressed upon us by nearly all who have written about the Christ and by nearly all who have attempted pictures of Him.

But let us not forget the other side, mirrored for us in the Gospels. He even got the name of being a frequenter of gay parties. He could have gone to the stodgiest modern Christmas Party and made it blaze with fun and happiness. He would have been " the life and soul of the party." " A gluttonous man," they said, " and a wine-bibber." How could a Man without humour be popular at parties? How could He be the kind of person to whom children run? How could it be said of Him that " the common people heard Him gladly "? I believe that if we had met the Master in the early days of His Galilean ministry we should have been struck by His gaiety, by His healthy laughter and the humour which bubbled up from His deep joy.

For when all has been said about joy, its opposite is not sorrow. Sorrow and joy can be held in the mind together at the same time. Of Jesus it is written, " Who for the joy that was set before Him endured the

Cross ", and the Cross was sorrowful enough. Again and again in our own experience, laughter and tears are close relatives in our family of feelings. True humour is only a temporary rising up of the deep sense that there is joy in the heart of the Universe. The opposite of joy is not sorrow. It is unbelief.

Claudel, the French poet, said that when he heard Beethoven's fifth symphony he knew that " there was eternal joy in the heart of the Universe ". And the New Testament, which is the most sorrowful book in the world, begins with the laughter of angels round the cradle of a Child, and ends with the Hallelujah Chorus sung by all the ransomed hosts of heaven.

After all, who has more right to humour than the Christian? The worldling may well be dismayed when his world is in pieces round him. For him humour may wither and die. But the Christian knows that the worth-while things cannot perish. He, too, sees the suffering and sin and sorrow of the world, and his laughter may often be silenced, but his joy no man taketh from him. For he has a gospel the scope of which makes room for the dark facts of life, its sin and sorrow and suffering, and he can say, not that all things work together for good to them that love God, but in the translation of those noble words which Professor Dodd offers us—" With those who love God, He—or God—co-operates in all things, for good."

So it is a Christian duty, as well as a privilege, from the deep well of joy which the Christian should still have when other wells have run dry, to meet the growing desert-barrenness of gloom and despondency about him, with the fresh and buoyant humour which faith makes possible.

There was a day when Christianity and gloom went together. Even the famous Cruden, whose concordance is on the shelves of most ministers, describes humour as follows : " To laugh ", he says, " is to be merry in a sinful manner." That was in 1769 ! Lord Chesterfield, who died in 1773, felt similarly.

" How low and unbecoming a thing laughter is," he says, " not to mention the disagreeable noise that it makes and the shocking contortion of the face that it occasions. "I am neither a melancholy man nor of cynical disposition . . . but I am sure that since I have had the full use of my reason nobody has ever heard me laugh."

We have learned to laugh since then. Even nonsense is a divine thing. G. K. Chesterton said, " The most important discovery of the Victorian age was that of nonsense." Children are still in many of our homes. One of the ways of saving them from the grim solemnity that is slowly overtaking some of us, as a horrid fog sweeps up a sunny hillside leaving hardly room for children to play, is to maintain a ministry of nonsense.

It is English to laugh. Let me quote some words of Earl Baldwin. " The English people have a curious sense of humour, rather than wit. Humour comes from the heart; wit comes from the brain. We can laugh at ourselves. Do you remember what Ruskin said? ' The English laugh is the purest and truest in the metals that can be minted '—and indeed only Heaven can know what the country owes to it. Laughter is one of the best things that God has given us and with hearty laughter neither malice nor indecency can exist." [1]

Yes, God has given it to us. He who has played with a baby or monkey or kitten or puppy has shared a joke with God. Humour is divine, and it is a true sense that makes us prefer a purely funny film to a purely doleful preacher. However dark our lot, let us remember the very English adage and " grin and bear it ", and if the worst comes to the worst let us be like the cat in " Alice in Wonderland ", and let the grin be the last thing to vanish.

For to laugh means that the happenings around us haven't got us down, that our faith is still victorious. The world *is* truly in a mess, but a joyous voice comes ringing down the centuries from a Man standing on the beach of a Galilean lake, with the sorrows of the world in His heart, but with the laughter of Heaven in His eyes, and He says, " Be of good cheer. I have overcome the world." Let us have faith in Him. For this is the victory that overcometh the world, even our faith.

[1] Stanley Baldwin, " The Torch I Hand on to You ", p. 89 (Hodder & Stoughton).

CHAPTER ELEVEN

PATIENCE

ONE OF THE REINFORCEMENTS OF FAITH
which we need most is patience. It is good
to have the glimpse of purpose and plan
which faith gives us, but what a lot of
patience we need to toil along the road
before the goal is reached !

One of the most thrilling passages in
Browning's " Paracelsus " is surely that in
which he tells how with flagging feet he
toiled onward, the goal out of sight, and
then how a vision of the city buoyed him
up and sent him on with reinforced faith,
patiently to struggle until he arrived.

> I remember well
> One journey, how I feared the track was missed,
> So long the city I desired to reach
> Lay hid; when suddenly its spires afar
> Flashed through the circling clouds; you may conceive
> My transport. Soon the vapours closed again,
> *But I had seen the city,* and one such glance
> No darkness could obscure :

Then comes the need of patience and he adds,

> Nor shall the present,
> A few dull hours, a passing shame or two,
> Destroy the vivid memories of the past.
> I will fight the battle out; a little spent
> Perhaps, but still an able combatant.

We need that patience now. The war drags on, and I know that I am writing about something that is relevant to our need, at any rate; the black-out nights, the dislocation of our ordinary activities and interests, perhaps the invasion of our homes by other folk, the strain of nightly bombardment, the lack of sleep and the vague fear and fretfulness which attack our minds, have meant for us a new need of patience.

This war has rightly been called a war of nerves : the insecurity of our job, perhaps, the sense of daily and nightly danger, the strain, day after day, of wondering what is happening to our loved ones, what may happen to them—indeed, what may happen to us all. All these things are putting a big demand on all our hearts.

I think that our own patience will be maintained better if we can consider the patience of God. I know that some of God's ministries are swift in their action. We think of the lightning, the earthquake, the tornado and the flood. These things descend upon man with terrific speed and violence, and there is much about them that we do not understand. But when our minds turn to the creative purposes of God, we find that the rule is that God works very slowly, very patiently. I suppose it is because He knows what He is doing, how it is all going to turn out, and that all His patience will prove worth-while.

> On every nest
> Where feathery Patience is content to brood
> And leaves her pleasure for the high emprize
> Of motherhood . . .
> There doth my Godhead rest.[1]

I remember some years ago, before I lived in London, taking an appointment on the south side of the River Thames and coming back to London to stay at a hotel for the night. I happened to walk along the northern bank of the river about midnight. In imagination I tried to see that great river in the far-off olden days, when it

[1] Evelyn Underhill.

flowed through the meadows, silently down
to the sea. I can't reproduce here the
spirit, the atmosphere, of that night. It
was a lovely, clear, frosty, dry, starlit
night, and London was sinking down to
quiet and rest, and I thought, as many
have thought before me, if that old river
could talk what a lot it could say to us all.
I recalled hearing Paul Robeson singing
the old negro song in " The Show Boat ",

> Ol' man river, dat ol' man river,
> He must know sumpin, but don't say nothin'
> He jes' keeps rollin', he keeps on rollin' along . . .
> Ah gits weary an' sick of tryin',
> Ahm tired of livin', and fear'd of dyin';
> But ol' man river he jes' keeps rollin' along.[1]

I thought of the days when the river
flowed through the wooded valleys and quiet
meadows down there by the Strand and
out through the marshes and into the sea.
As I passed, on the Embankment, Cleopatra's Needle—that monument that goes
back into the dim mists of history—I
remembered Sir James Jeans saying that if
you stuck a postage stamp on the top of
Cleopatra's Needle, then the thickness of

[1] Oscar Hammerstein.

the stamp compared with the height of
Cleopatra's Needle would give you an indi-
cation of the length of time man had been
on the earth compared with the time during
which there had been an earth. I have
read that if one divided the history of this
world into 7,000 equal parts, then during
the first 6,999 there would be no sign of man.

> This fine old world of ours is but a child
> Yet in the go-cart.   Patience !   Give it time
> To learn its limbs : there is a Hand that guides.

How patiently God prepared for man !
Some tell us that He took two thousand
million years to prepare a home for man.

I like to think of all those processes that
make it possible for a gaily-coloured butter-
fly to develop from the caterpillar, emerge
from its chrysalis and rise up into the sunshine. Yet in one day that tiny fragment
of beautiful life has lived its span, fulfilled
its purpose and passed away. All that
patient preparation for so small a thing, so
short a life, makes me very ashamed of my
impatience.

There is no adequate human illustration
of that kind of thing. The nearest, per-

haps, is the patient building of a great cathedral, such as that at Liverpool. The architect, who was just a young man of twenty-one when his plans were accepted, dimly hopes, if he is spared, that the cathedral may be somewhere near completion before he dies. The only other human illustration that attracts me is that lovely story of the American tourist who went to Oxford. He was strolling through the gardens of one of the Colleges and said to the gardener, " How do you get these lawns like this? " The old gardener looked at him and said, " Well, sir, you see, we just waters them, and mows them and rolls them, and waters them and mows them and rolls them, and waters them and mows them and rolls them for eight hundred years, and then they are like that." And the American said, " Well, I guess I had better go back to New York and begin."

When we think of those processes which have paved the way for beautiful things, how the patience of God stands out against our impatience ! It is our impatience which makes it seem to us that God doesn't answer prayer. There cannot be such a thing as an unanswered prayer. If you were a father and your little child tugged your coat and said, " Daddy, I want . . .", you would not push him away. You would not avert your face and look the other way and assume a stony stare. You might not be able to give him what he wanted, but you would pick him up in your arms and love him. How stupid it must really be to talk about unanswered prayer ! If God is a Father and God is love, and you are His child, there cannot be such a thing as a refusal to answer. I am sure this patient, loving God is whispering to our hearts, " Wait ! wait ! " That is a very hard lesson for man to learn. God is more patient than man dreams credible. Man's refusal to believe in God's patience, in my view, accounts for the form which the Story of the Flood took. Some local calamity there probably was. But it was incredible to godly men in those days, that the God who was holy and omnipotent could put up any longer with man's sins and futilities. So an ancient happening became a legend which taught that God just wiped the slate clean of dirty human nature, " drowned the

lot ", save a select few, and started again.
That is man making God in his own image.
Man making a mental concept of an impatient God because he didn't believe God
could possibly bear with men any longer.

When I look at my own heart with its
incessant appeals for forgiveness and its endless new beginnings, I am amazed that God
can stand me any longer : I am still more
surprised that He can stand some people I
know ! Perhaps it was an inability to
accept the thought of God's infinite patience
that led the Calvinists into some harsh
doctrines. The Calvinists tried to understand why nine-tenths of the people did
not care for God, so they said it must be
that God does not will to save them. They
are not the chosen ones, God has no time
for them—as we say. " Why doesn't God
make man repent ? " asked the Calvinists ;
and since there seemed to be no answer,
then, said the Calvinists, it must be that He
does not want them. So, out of their own
impatience, they made a false mental image
of God as dangerously misleading as a false
metal image of God.

I remember hearing my predecessor in

o

Leeds, Rev. A. E. Whitham, who now has gone into the great silence, say, " If I were God I think I would have a brass plate on the door ; at any rate I would make people's ears burn, I would teach them to show me due respect." But I am glad he was not God though I loved and admired him ! The real God does not strive or cry or let His voice be heard in the streets. He does not hustle men into decisions or hurry their mental processes. Love is very patient, very kind. Theodore Parker said, " The trouble is that God is not in a hurry, and I am." That is the trouble with a lot of us. Many of us are saying in our hearts, " If I were God I would teach Hitler where he got off. I would not let him do this, that and the other. Why doesn't God do something ? " The poet Whittier said as he fought for freedom for the slaves, " I confess when I think of the atrocities of slavery, I am almost ready to call fire from Heaven."

Perhaps impatience is the key to the character of Judas. One must not here attempt to work out his psychology. But it is hard to suppose that after nearly three

years with Jesus he could go and sell Him
for £5. After all, if he had been mainly a
money-grabber, he wouldn't have joined a
band of penniless preachers, and he would
have secured a far bigger sum than thirty
pieces of silver.

But Judas was impatient with God, as
war is making many of us now. He had
seen Jesus raise the dead, heal the sick and
do many mighty works. He had seen a fire
kindle in men's eyes when Jesus spoke.
He thought Jesus could overthrow Rome
if He set Himself to do it. " Why ", said
Judas to himself, " if I had a tenth of His
power I wouldn't waste another moment.
Why doesn't He *act*? " So Judas thrust
Jesus into a corner in which he thought the
Master would act. He tried to force the
hand of Jesus. He never dreamed that a
man who raised the dead would let Himself
be taken. . . . How many feel the same today ! Why doesn't God *do* something ?

But Judas only hastened his Master's
journey to the Cross. God knows the way
that He takes. It may be the way that
costs us and Him most, but there are no
short cuts. A patient God treads His own

Via Dolorosa, and asks us to share His patience and His sorrow because only along that road can He bring humanity home to its final crowning with all the values safe.

Some lovely lines of G. K. Chesterton come to the mind :—

> To an open house in the evening
> Home shall men come,
> To an older place than Eden
> And a taller town than Rome;
> To the end of the way of the wandering star,
> To the things that cannot be and that are,
> To the place where God was homeless
> And all men are at home.

It is often a long way home, but it is better than a short cut to a mere lodging-house.

I think there was a time when even Jesus was tempted to be impatient. As I try imaginatively to watch Him out there in the desert, after the Baptism, when He knew that He stood in a unique relationship with God, out there in the great silence, as He watched the great planets wheel in the sky, as He lived among wild beasts for over a month in prayer and self-discipline, I catch a glimpse of that patience in which He won His soul. He was thinking out His programme. He did *so* want to get the ear of the people. What was the way to do it? The flat stones looked like the loaves His mother made, and as He saw them He said, " Yes, my people are starving, my people won't listen to me yet. If I bring in a new order of things, so that there is food for these hungry people to eat, then they will listen to me." He could have brought about social reform. It would have been a quick way to get the ear of the people, but it did not fit in with God's way. It was a short cut. It was buying men's allegiance with bread. So He put it behind Him. You cannot change hearts by providing bread and there is no progress without changed hearts.

The inner voice of impatience said, " You could float down from the pinnacle of the Temple, you could do wonderful things; nothing arouses the enthusiasm of people so much as a person who will work magic." Then, as He thought it all out in the light of the patience of God, He knew that miracles must never be worked to make a short cut to men's hearts. So He put that behind Him too. No miracles were worked to make men say " Isn't He wonderful? " You cannot change men's hearts with magic. They will be amazed and follow from curiosity and then go on as before. And there is no progress without changed hearts.

The voice of impatience tried again: " Never mind, the country is ripe for revolution; lift your finger and a thousand men will bring their swords. You could claim all the kingdoms of this Jewish world. They are looking for a King." Then He knew that that would not do either. You cannot buy men with patriotism if you want them for God, because God's Kingdom is bigger than that and takes in all kingdoms. God's Kingdom is the Kingdom of the changed heart. Nationalism is frequently its greatest enemy.

There was something born in the desert that day: a new patriotism, the idea of a greater kingdom, where *all* should be brothers and *all* the children of God. And that is going to take a long time, it is going to take all the patience of God, for He must wait for the tardy co-operation of men. So Jesus put it away from Him.

He knew there were no short cuts. In patience He had won His soul.

Do you remember the picture of the man sowing tares in an enemy's field, and how the human remedy was immediate action to root them up? But Jesus said, " Let them grow together until the harvest." [1]

Do you remember this word about God? " For He maketh his sun to rise on the evil and on the good, and sendeth rain on the just and on the unjust." [2]

Do you remember the day when the disciples were with Jesus in a Samaritan village and the Samaritans would not listen to Him and the disciples said, " Lord, wilt thou that we bid fire to come down from heaven, and consume them? " [3] But Jesus said, " You don't understand." They didn't understand the patience of God; and all through the Gospels it is the same story.

Do you sometimes at a Communion Service shut your eyes and go back in imagination to that long, low, upper room, and see the lamp swaying in the evening breeze, and the disciples reclining at the

[1] Matt. 13³⁰.　　[2] Matt. 5⁴⁵.　　[3] Luke 9⁵⁴.

table only eighteen inches high? Do you
feel the sense of indescribable sorrow? Do
you almost hear Judas's sandals scraping
over the floor as he leaves and makes for
the doorway? If those disciples had known
what he was going to do, they would have
stood between him and the door, even
killed him, rather than let him do what
he was going to do; but Jesus said, " What
you are going to do, do quickly." How
patient Jesus is! Those disciples could not
take in the thoughts of Christ about His
Kingdom. They wanted quick action,
quick results. They thought that there
would be a king reigning and they themselves on thrones around him. Do you remember how the mother of two of them
was so anxious about those thrones that she
wanted one of her sons to be on the right
hand and the other on the left when the
King came in his kingdom? But when He
came in His Kingdom, His throne was a
Cross and on His right and on His left
were two thieves. What a long way round
to a kingdom! But that is the way He
took us. He is taking us that way again,
and we must share His patience.

In an old-fashioned novel the heroine asks her uncle this question, " What does one end by doing when all the best is taken away from one, when life has grown trivial, stunted and narrow; when the sun of one's happiness is set ? "—And here is the wise answer of an old man : " After a time, Polly, not at once—that would be asking too much of poor human nature— but after a time, my dear, one lights a candle called Patience, and guides one's footsteps by that."

Well, if we are wise, and are determined to come out of this war spiritually victorious, we shall add to our faith patience. We shall not wait too long before we light such a candle.   For this is the day of blackouts in more senses than one. When Viscount Grey, then Sir Edward Grey, Britain's Foreign Secretary, saw, in the summer of 1914, that war was inevitable, he stood at the window of the Foreign Office and said, in a voice that no one who heard it will ever forget, " The lamps are going out all over Europe." I wonder what that lovely soul would say today !—Even to youth I would say : ' Light your candle.   You have started out to train for a career in hope of a joyous life, full of service to the community, and now your progress, perhaps your very existence, is threatened.   Light a candle of patience.' To many in middle life with a reasonable sense of security I would say : ' Light your candle.   The security of anything in this world is overshadowed by a great darkness.' To those in old age I would say : ' Light your candle, for the light of a candle of patience lit at the burning love of Christ may be the only light for you at eventide.'

We all need patience. The nervous tension caused by war makes us jumpy and irritable. Trifles at which we should have laughed in the old, care-free days can upset us out of all proportion to their importance. We hurt even our dearest by a sharp word or cutting remark.

The chaotic condition of transport, which used to run so smoothly and up to time, doesn't breed patience. The waiting, the rushing for bus or tube, having to fight a good fight to get in at all—these activities make us impatient with others, hectic and short-tempered.

The awful, grim struggle, to which at

present (December 1940) we can see no end, makes us impatient. We view the cost in men, in money, in nervous health with dismay. We wonder whether ever again will come the old, lovely, happy, care-free days we once enjoyed. . . .

No wonder we pray for patience. Perhaps I may quote Viscount Grey again. Writing to Margot Asquith he said :—[1]

" DEAR MRS. ASQUITH,

I can really say nothing in answer to your letter. There is suffering which purifies, raises, and strengthens, and in which one can see the Crown as well as the Cross ; but where there is no Crown visible it is terrible even to see suffering, and it must be intolerable to undergo it. My own belief is that if we could know all we should understand everything, but there is much in the world that cannot be explained without knowing what came before life and what is to come after it, and of that we know nothing, for faith is not knowledge.

[1] " The Autobiography of Margot Asquith ", Vol. 2, p. 91.

All that we can do is to take refuge in reverence and submission. ' God is in Heaven and thou upon earth, therefore let thy words be few ' is one way of expressing the reverence, and : ' I was dumb and opened not my mouth, for it was Thy doing ' is an expression of submission. They are hard things to say, but I don't know what else is to be said and it is better to say them than to rail against what we cannot understand, or to attempt to belittle it, and put a gloss upon it."

In that lovely letter there breathes the spirit of the New Testament word " Patience ". It is not a passive word. It is a dynamic word. " Let us *run* with patience," says the author of the letter to the Hebrews, not " Let us sit with patience ". Patience is often pictured with folded hands. Not so in the New Testament. The sentence of Jesus—" In your patience ye shall win your souls," is translated by Dr. Moffat thus : " Hold out stedfast and you win your souls." [1]

St. Luke uses the word (8[15]) in the

----

[1] Luke 21[19].

elucidation of the Parable of the Sower.
The seed on the good ground brings forth
fruit with patience, and bringing forth
fruit involves—does it not?—activity : taking something from the rain, the sun, the
soil, and turning it into fruit. Every vine
knows how to turn the water into wine !
Yet, in spite of activity, growth is a matter
of patience. You may fume and fret at
the long winter, but you can do nothing to
hurry the spring. Activity and patience
are not opposites, but complements.

It is of God's ordaining, this slowness in
the *growth* of the most worth-while things.
The sudden conversion? Yes, but the
finest souls know that while they are at the
end of their wandering, they are only at
the beginning of their journey. The sudden
flash of lightning may rend the mountain
peak and leave a scar, but that sudden
cleft only provides the opportunity for
tiny seeds to find lodgement. Day after
day mountain mists must kiss the hard
crag with their cool, fertilising breath ;
a whole season of rain and shine must pass
before the cleft can fill with those tiny wild
flowers—the mountain pansy, the vetch,

the pimpernel, which the mountain wears as proudly as a woman the gems of her beloved.

Everyone who has learned a language—including his own—knows what I mean by patience which is active as well as passive. Everyone who plays an instrument well knows how much work and how much patience are needed. Everyone who has *learned* to do anything well, from running a home to ruling a country, knows the stern demand on patience.

We shan't expect to escape in our religious life, shall we? For myself, I know that I've done nothing yet but make the poorest kind of start, with faltering and failure and many turnings back, but I am determined on one thing : I won't give up. If He were any ordinary kind of Leader, He would have given me up long ago, but His patience and love are far greater than mine. I have His promise : " I will never leave you nor forsake you. Him that cometh to Me I will in no wise cast out." I'm going to cling to those promises. I want to hold on until, in my own life and that of this great nation, I can see God working out His plans.

And when I'm tempted to be impatient with my own progress and tempted to give the whole thing up, I'm going to take a look at Jesus, and remember that if I miss— what I believe to be the most wonderful experience a human being can ever have— a saving experience of His love, it won't be His fault, but mine. So, I'll run with patience, looking unto Jesus, the Author and Perfecter of faith.

I'll take a look at Jesus, too, when I'm tempted to be impatient with others. They can't try me a tenth as much as I try the patience of Christ. And so often, I find, I'm impatient with people because I just don't understand what is happening in their hearts and minds.

Here's a true story to illustrate what I mean. The chef on a luxury liner used to delight the passengers by making the cakes for tea and the ices for dinner in the most attractive shapes. One might find a little cake like a basket of fruit. One might find an ice-cream in the form of a model of the ship. One day the little cakes were not as " cute " as usual, and an American girl complained accordingly. She didn't know that while the vessel slipped through the sunny seas it was taking the chef further and further from a wife who was desperately ill. The American spoilt darling didn't know that when the chef was trying to do better in consequence of the complaint that was passed on to him, he got a wireless message to say that his dearest was dead.

I knew of a school in the north in which every boy who was late was caned without being given any opportunity of offering an explanation. One morning a master severely thrashed a lad for lateness, only to find afterwards that the late-comer had been at the pit-head all night waiting for news of his brother who was trapped underground in a coal-mine and who was subsequently brought out dead. The story —which I verified—came to me when I was engaged in a Press campaign against caning in schools which cost me much opposition and abuse. One's blood boils at the incident, but I wonder what our own impatience has cost others—and God!

I'll take a look at Jesus when I'm tempted to lose patience with God and say to Him, " Why did you ever make such a world if you can't run it better than this ? " " God is in Heaven, thou upon earth; therefore let thy words be few." Yes, there's wisdom there. All this sorrow and loss and worry and pain. . . . But He *knew* it was possible, that it would come—and He went on building and planning and trusting men.

Two dear friends of mine, an elderly man and his wife, were going with my sister to see Liverpool Cathedral. As they examined the exterior, the old lady said, as she poked at the stone with her umbrella, " I think they have chosen the wrong kind of stone. It's pretty, but it's too soft. It won't last." To which, with a twinkle in his eye, her husband answered, " Yes, dear; but, you know, I expect the architect thought of that ! "

How we complain about God's world ! Why didn't He do this and that? We forget that nine-tenths of its misery has come because man has gone wrong at this point or that. And for the rest, and indeed for the possibility of all the sorrow and suffering in all the world, we may say

P

reverently, 'The Architect of the Universe thought of that.'

When I look at the Cross, I say to myself very quietly—and a strange awe and hush comes upon me—" He thought of that." He knew it would cost that. And He went on because He had enough patience to believe that it was worth even that. And He who hung there—He who, so pure and innocent, might have railed at God and called the Universe a failure, a devilish fraud, a foul obscenity—called God *Father*, and died in unbroken peace. And all the saints in their own way, and so many of them at cost of everything that human lives count dear, followed that lead.

We are just to walk quietly along each day's road with persevering patience, looking unto Jesus, and leaving responsibility to God. He has thought of everything that can happen to us. You may have every reason for impatience. An income cut down yet again; little children perhaps thrust upon you even while your own are far away; a difficult husband; a sense of insecurity in your job and the awful strain of what may never come; the threat to your dear ones, your homes and lives and existence. . . . He knoweth the way that you take. He has thought of that !

None of us will ever have to face a situation which has not been faced by those who love Christ. In imagination I sometimes see the roof of the City Temple roll back, and a multitude of the heavenly host praising God with us and looking down on us with great love and with shining eyes, hoping desperately that we shan't—in our day and generation—let things down.

Therefore let us also, seeing we are compassed about with so great a cloud of witnesses, lay aside every weight and the sin which doth so easily beset us, and let us run with patience the race that is set before us, looking unto Jesus, the Author and Perfecter of our Faith, the faith in which alone the spirit finds its victory. "This is the victory that overcometh the world, even our faith."

CHAPTER TWELVE

HOPE

I HAVE WRITTEN AT LENGTH ABOUT FAITH and a little about patience. I should like to write a few words about hope, although perhaps the equation might be allowed.

$$\text{Faith} + \text{Patience} = \text{Hope}.$$

"We are saved by hope," says St. Paul.[1] It is a great word, and it occurs many times in the New Testament. It is a matter for regret that this great word has been used in a weak way to mean merely wishful thinking. "I hope it will clear up," we say about the weather. Or, conventionally to a friend, "I hope you'll have a good holiday." We have even debased the word below such kindly, well-meaning phrases, and half-humorously have said, "You've got a hope!" or "Some hope!"

But the word "hope" in the Bible is a

[1] Rom. 8[24].

228

virile, strong, dynamic, soldierly word. It
is part of the armour of the Christian,[1]
preventing him from being smitten down. I
should define it as " a firm expectation of
promised blessing ", and perhaps in the
equation printed above we ought to add
Love to Patience and Faith. We have
that firm expectation because we believe in
the nature of that Person in whose hands are
all things—all the destinies of men and
nations.

If I could paint, and tried to illustrate the
trinity of Faith, Hope and Love, I should
paint Faith as a strong man, serene, quiet,
confident, ready for hardship and sacrifice.
I should paint Love as a tender woman with
strong character in the eyes and mouth,
ready to suffer and endure. I should paint
Hope as their child, vigorous, buoyant,
straining towards the future, smiling. And
round all three figures I should have a vivid
blue light or some other symbol that implied
that all lived fully only in God.

For when Paul uses the phrase, " having
no hope and without God in the world," [2]
we feel that the two phrases mean the same

[1] I Thess. 5[8].   [2] Ephes. 2[12].

thing.   As our first chapter sought to show, there is little or no progress apart from God, and no hope that the fair dreams of man can ever come true.

When the Psalmist wrote, " Hope thou in God," [1] he gave to the world the only ground for hope that exists.

Is that too strong a thing to say ?   I think not, for without God man is a highly cultured animal functioning a planet. But with God man is a spirit functioning the eternal, unseen, spiritual universe, the true and enduring " world without end " to which we refer at the end of so many prayers and which we so imperfectly understand.

The highest things in human personality do not function if you take away from man all that we mean by the spiritual. Since we have embarked on equations, we might try a few in the religious field. Saul the persecutor plus God equals Paul the valiant tireless missionary. Sensual Augustine plus God equals Saint Augustine. John Wesley the unkindled, conventional Church-of-England clergyman plus God equals a

[1] Psalm 42[11].

blazing torch that set all England on fire with religious revival in the eighteenth century.

I see no hope of progress while man uses his discoveries, inventions and gifts for selfish ends; but what amazing visions flash into the mind as one contemplates great statesmen, great scientists, great artists, great economists, great business leaders, great civil servants all aflame with love for God and a passion to interpret their particular job in His spirit and in terms of His Kingdom ! Faith and Love together give birth to such a hope, and such a hope is " a firm expectation of promised blessing ". " I *will* pour out my Spirit on all flesh and your young men *shall* see visions and your old men dream dreams." [1]

We sometimes speak disparagingly of human nature, but it would seem a frustration of God's purposes, as well as human hopes, if that lowly yet august thing we call human nature were denied its perfect functioning; if this earth, born from the burning womb of the sun and prepared

[1] Acts 2[17].

through so many æons to be man's birth-place, should produce a creature which stopped before all the high possibilities of its earth-bound nature were realised.

If this present catastrophe is, as some think, the end of the world, the Christian has no cause for dismay, for all that is essentially man—namely, his spirit—goes on to live and work in a spiritual existence. What a thrill it must have been to the convert from paganism to realise that for the Christian there is always a future ! In the case of the pagan there was only a future for youth. Old age looked back. There was nothing ahead. Tragedy, in that setting, especially for youth, was ap-palling. It was the end of all things. But the Christian drama lifted an impene-trable curtain. If life ended through either old age or calamity, there was now a further horizon. The word " hope " had a new and undreamt-of significance. As the letter of St. Peter written about A.D. 65 to the distressed folk in Rome who were being bitterly persecuted by Nero, said, " He begat us again into *a living hope*, by the resurrection of Jesus Christ from the dead." The door of hope is no longer closed if friends die, funds fail, or death threatens. Clouds lift and reveal far-off horizons.

" Call the world, if you please, ' the vale of soul making '," said Keats in one of his letters, " and then you will find out the use of the world." We may part with the world and our life on it just as a boy parts with his first Latin primer when, later on, he can revel in reading Horace's " Odes ". The earth-life has not been wasted if it is only a preparatory school and if the university course of the soul lies completely in the next—or spiritual—phase of life.

At the same time if man will only take God into his reckoning, he has every ground for hoping that his earth-bound dreams may yet actualise. He hopes for a Kingdom of Heaven on earth. He longs to see the earth become what it would become if all the possibilities of human nature were realised. It could be free from disease, from sweating, from slums, from crippling poverty, from immorality, from despair and hopelessness, from that fatigue and burden in work which rob it of its high-purpose—namely, the joy of creative activity.

We sometimes speak of human nature as if these things could never come to pass. Human nature is certainly fundamentally evil. But it is the purpose of God that it should be redeemed, that His own life should so enter it, empower it and direct it, that those energies which flow now so often in selfish channels should flow down the slopes of divine grace with far greater momentum and in the channels of loving service and creative expression.

If and when they do this, they will not be less human, but more so. We judge things by their best, not by their worst. Was Saul less a man after his conversion? Was John Wesley less truly human when he flamed through the country calling men to God than when he lived that far less significant life in Georgia?

The gardener takes the rough briar from the hedge and grafts into it the life of a finer rose. Forthwith the engrafted plant brings forth quite different flowers, infinitely superior, which formerly it could never have produced. Has the briar become less essentially rose-like? Has it not rather risen to its highest capabilities? " That is what

a real rose can be," we say. So when man
lets God into his life fully, by surrender to
the Divine inflow, he is not less man, but
more. "Abide in Me," said Christ. "I
am the Vine, ye are the branches. As the
branch cannot bear fruit of itself except it
abide in the Vine, so neither can ye except
ye abide in Me. . . . Apart from Me ye can
do nothing." [1]

In those words alone stands the con-
demnation of humanism. Jesus Himself
seems to have despaired of seeing progress
come through unredeemed man, but to have
had solid hope in those glorious possibilities
which can actualise if man will only rise to
his true stature by opening up his life to God.

Let us not talk, then, the defeatist nonsense that there will always be wars because
it is human nature to fight, that there will
always be slums because it is human nature
to be selfish, and so on, but rather see
human nature as Christ revealed it and as
He can make it. Given man's acceptance
of God's offer, human nature, using well all
it has learnt already, developing further
all the resources at its disposal, could, in a

[1] John 15[4].

very short period, rise up and expel everything that now curses our life together.

In doing so it would not cease to be human, any more than the cultivated rose ceases to be a rose, or the luscious grape ceases to be the fruit of the vine when it develops from the bitter berry of the hedgerow from which it took its origin, or the apple ceases to be an apple when, from the bitter crab of the woods, it emerges as the lovely pippin.

As to whether our hopes will be realised *on earth*, everything depends on whether God is really received and interpreted in man's life. If not, in spite of all our vaunted progress, our cleverness, our conferences, our schemes for amelioration, our whole civilisation, our whole world-life will be tossed on one side as being unusable by the Divine hand.

I heard a moving and true story recently. Try to picture the scene. It was Christmas Eve in a middle-class home. There was no poverty, no real need. Three children had gone to bed. But they were much too excited to sleep. They did not believe any longer in Father Christmas, but they did believe in Daddy. Their mother, too, had given them reason to hope. Daddy had promised that when he was up in town he would get the presents which were to fill their stockings.

Then, very late, there was the sound of unsteady feet and a rough voice which they hardly recognised. Daddy was drunk. He had spent all his money on drink. He had completely forgotten his children. When he got home it was too late to do anything about it, and he was much too fuddled, even if a shop here and there had still been open. The mother could do nothing. The next morning three little stockings were empty. The children crept together into one bed and wept their disappointment out under the bedclothes. Having dressed, they loyally tried to keep back further tears, tried to behave as though nothing had happened, tried to love the one who had brought such disappointment to their home. They had hoped, they had had reason to hope, but the character of the person concerned, the character which was the basis of their hopes, had broken down.

Jesus said it was legitimate to argue from

a human father to God where fatherly rela-
tionships are concerned. We know that the
nature of God is beyond all our dreaming
and guessing and thinking. There must be
qualities in His being which we haven't the
wit to understand. Truly He does things
and allows things which confuse and be-
wilder us—lightning, tornado, earthquake
and the *extent* and horror of evil as it affects
us now with our little vision. I confess I
often need to summon all my faith to hold
fast to Him.

Then I come to my senses by remembering that He would not put us in a world
which carries so many arguments against
Him unless He could answer them all.
And I cannot believe He will disappoint us
at last. We shan't be confounded at last.
" If *ye* then," said Jesus, " know how to
give good gifts to your children, how much
more will He give ! " [1]   God bewilders us
more than a good father bewilders his
children. They are near enough in equality
to him—especially as they grow older—to
understand. We can't expect to understand all God does and allows just now.

[1] Matt. 7[11].

But He would be no God, but worse than a drunken fiend, if He let us hope as He encourages us to do, and made us promises, and then finally threw our hope back in our faces and laughed at us for being credulous fools. " Hope thou in God, for I shall yet praise Him." The character of God as Jesus revealed Him is the basis of that firm expectation of blessing which we call hope.

We will take our stand with that brave soul who made a list of his adversities and trials : " Five times received I forty stripes save one, thrice was I beaten with rods, once was I stoned, thrice I suffered shipwreck, a night and a day have I been in the deep, in journeyings often, in perils of rivers, in perils of robbers. . . ." [1] What a list ! And what a human thing to do, to make such a list ! But he who through all his trials carried with him through the darkness the bright lamp of a burning hope wrote some words to the Romans [2] of which Dr. Moffatt has given a glorious translation.

NO ONE WHO BELIEVES IN HIM WILL EVER BE DISAPPOINTED—NO ONE.

---

[1] 2 Cor. 11^{25} ff.   [2] Rom. 10$^{11-12}$.

CHAPTER THIRTEEN

TRUTH

WHAT A TREMENDOUS SUPPORT TO FAITH IS to be found in the thought that finally truth will prevail. The minutiae of faith may have to be adapted and readapted; the things believed about God may have to be expressed in different language; every generation will talk about God in terms of its own " isms " and " ologies " and thought-forms. But the bases of faith are solidly built up from bed-rock truth.

I remember reading of a young woman who kept house for her mother and father over a long period of years. It so happened that she kept the tea in a tin which bore on its lid a picture of the Rock of Gibraltar. Several times each day she saw the picture of this Rock. It was as familiar as anything could be.

At thirty-two years of age her circumstances changed and she found herself on

board a P. & O. liner going out to Egypt.
One sunny morning she wakened, looked
out of the port-hole, and there was the
Rock of Gibraltar just as it had been pictured on the tea-tin. Here are her actual
words, " There rising up, almost within the
toss of a ship's biscuit, was Gibraltar Rock,
just as I had heard of it and seen it pictured
scores of times; but heavens! it was REAL.
I almost cried out, ' Then it has been real,
like that, all the time.' " She could take
a small boat, land, get her feet on the *real
rock*.

Many of us in these days are shaken to
the depths. Life was proceeding happily,
business was not good, but we didn't worry
about it. Health was normal. Prospects
were satisfactory. Our children were growing up happily. We had dreams about
them and made plans for them. But now
that glory has departed. For some, business worries are acute, nervous health is
threatened, children, perhaps, are away
from home; we seem to be living on a short
lease which we feel may end abruptly. The
old security has gone. No one knows what
will happen. Perhaps our boys are fighting

Q

already.   Perhaps tonight our home will be destroyed by a bomb, our dear ones and ourselves killed.

Spiritually we need nothing so much as the feel of a rock under our feet. Our religion, perhaps, does not give us that sense of security. It is like the picture of the Rock on a tea-tin. We are familiar with it. We are not irreligious. We say our prayers. We believe in God. We attend services and sing hymns. We want our children to be religious. We are sure that religion has value. We have had moments ourselves of re-dedication.   But, however familiar, our religion is a picture more than a reality, our faith is vague, wishful thinking, not built up securely from the rock of truth.

Can we follow a road of thought which will help us to get our feet on the rock?

When I was in Palestine six years ago, the outstanding impression made on my mind was that of the solid foundation, the unshakeable, unassailable rock, on which Christianity is built. The Indian religions wind back into labyrinthine ways and lose you at last in a desert of myth and story.

In Palestine you listen to the guide telling you all sorts of queer stories that you can't believe. (One guide showed me the footprint of Adam in the rocky floor of a cave! I never knew before that our first parent had such big feet.) But however unbelievable some of the stories may be, yet amongst the welter of legend, and the conglomeration of accounts which no one could weave into a single whole, there stands the unassailable FACT of a life lived which has by now influenced every country in the world. The Christian Faith is based on fact, built up from the living rock of Truth.

One lovely summer evening stands out clearly in my memory. We had visited the limestone cave in which, they tell you, Christ was born. The air was heavy with incense, the place lighted with no less than fifty-three lamps. We listened to the stories the guide told us of the endless quarrelling that goes on between Greeks and Armenians and Roman Catholics. On one nail the Catholics can hang a picture. On another the Greeks can do the same. The third is a neutral nail on which nothing can be hung without precipitating a crisis! Always in the place where the Prince of Peace is said to have been born, a policeman stands on duty.

We were nauseated by the dark, smelly place. Then we came out into the sunshine, went down through the narrow streets of Bethlehem to the Shepherds' Field. " The sheep with their little lambs passed us by on the road." We sat down amongst the flowers and watched the sun go down behind Bethlehem. I can see it now. After the flaming colours had died, the sky turned a daffodil yellow, with the towers and minarets of Bethlehem standing out black against it. The evening star shone in trembling glory. The bell from the mosque " stumbled on sudden music and was still ". One by one lights peeped out in Bethlehem. A dog barked, a man shouted. Then stillness and the hush of night. . . .

In my heart dawned a great sense of certainty, the hush of a great strength, a great feeling of security. Somewhere near where we sat amid the flowers, a life began on earth —it didn't matter exactly where or how—a life in which God was utterly trusted at

every step. That life was real, as real as
Gibraltar. It wasn't a myth, a story, a
beautiful picture. It was a fact of history.
No lies of futile guides, no silly legends or
tawdry tales could menace that fact, any
more than a child's squib could blow up
Gibraltar. Tacitus, Pliny, Josephus, his-
torians with no axe to grind, have all paid
their tribute to the great, unassailable,
invulnerable, eternal truth that that Life
which began at Bethlehem has been lived
out in a place which could still be visited.
Let us start with the fact of Christ.

Further, equally unassailable are the
records of what He said and did and was.
In their main essentials those records agree.
Recently a man or two men interrupted
one of our broadcast services from the City
Temple. I couldn't pretend to tell you
what the men said, because I tried to concentrate on continuing what I was saying.
But I received cuttings from more than
half-a-dozen newspapers which purported
to report what the men said. Members of
the congregation had been interviewed and
so on. There were not two newspapers
which had exactly the same account of

what was said. Yet they were published the day after the event they described.

I am greatly impressed by the fact that though St. Mark, the earliest Gospel, was not written for at least thirty years after the death of Christ, we are given a picture of Him consistent with itself, and, in all essentials, consistent with other records from other sources.

The white light of criticism, some of it hostile, has beaten on those records for two thousand years, yet Christ stands out, His words and deeds and life unassailable, so that we, in the twentieth century, know more of Him than any generation save His own. To *invent* what He said and did and was would require His equal in character and insight.

But let us pass on. His Resurrection is equally unassailable, equally real. I am not now concerned with its manner or explanation. What happened to His body, to my mind, matters no more than what happened to His clothes. But certainly nothing less than the certainty that all that was essential in Jesus of Nazareth had survived death could have changed those timid men, hiding in fear of their lives, into bold missionaries who, within seven weeks of His crucifixion, *when anyone could have produced contrary evidence if it were to be had*, were preaching His Resurrection, in the very city where He had been done to death; men who later died rather than deny that affirmation.

Those men claimed to be in living touch with Him. " Our fellowship is with the Father and with His Son Jesus Christ,"[1] they proudly claimed. His Ascension was not good-bye, for they returned from it, we are told, with great joy.[2] They *knew* He was still with them.[3] They laid no flowers on His grave. No one ever wrote memorial verses about Him. You don't do that for One who is still there and REAL and radiantly, actively alive !

Now, at what point in history can we put down our finger and say, " After this, no one ever had communion with Christ again "? There is no such point. The Ascension may have marked the end of His communion *through the senses* with most of His followers. But to say communion with Christ ended

[1] 1 John 1³.   [2] Luke 24⁵⁰⁻⁵³.   [3] Mark 16¹⁹⁻²⁰

then, makes nonsense of the era which opened with the Acts of the Apostles, nonsense of the lives of the saints, nonsense of the faith of tens of thousands of fine men and women who have left all and dared all for His sake, and who, both in our own land and in India and China and Africa and the isles of the sea, will, through the power of their communion with Him, be casting out this very day the devils of ignorance and disease and sin.

All this is of tremendous importance for modern faith. Whether we cast our eyes to wide horizons or focus them here at home in this country, or more closely, perhaps, if we focus them on our own hearts and lives and those of our fellows, we find trouble and tempest everywhere. There are not wanting those who warn us of still greater perils to come. Altogether there is sufficient cause for us to make sure that we have an anchor, and that that anchor is fixed on a Rock that cannot be moved. When an old Scottish saint lay dying, his daughter approached his bed and said, " Will I read a chapter to ye, Father? " " Na, na, lassie," he said, " the storm's up noo; I theekit (thatched)

ma hoose in calm weather." For many of
us the storm is now raging, but behind the
demand for faith is the Rock of Truth.

Truth, Beauty and Goodness, the philosophers tell us, are ultimates. Without
much philosophical training we know a
little of what they mean. There is something final about them—something which
defies analysis. When they are perceived
by the mind and spirit, a harbour is found
where the personality can rest.

These ultimate truths are reached, not by
intellectual processes only, or by the authority of another, but by intuitive recognition
as well. This is more clearly illustrated
when we are thinking of beauty and goodness. We do not need ten reasons for supposing that a lily is beautiful. A dawn seen
from some Alpine height needs no argument
to prove it beautiful. A kind and unselfish
act does not need argument to make us see
it as an expression of goodness. Yet arguments help. The work of a great master
may only appear beautiful after our intellect has been engaged and we have been
taught how to look at it. The goodness of
our parents in their disciplining of our

characters may need a good deal of argument before we appreciate it as good!

So truth may sometimes require argument before it can possess us, but, when it does, we recognise that something has happened within us beside the effect of arguments carried through to their logical finality. Something within us leaps out, as it does when we recognise beauty and goodness, and we say, "That is true." Truth then becomes what Shelley called "a truth of the emotions". We *feel* it true as well as see it true, and until then truth has no power to hold the ship of our life steady in the storm.

Yet this is no disparagement of the approach to truth through reason or through experiment, observation and inference, or through philosophical quest. Indeed, the Church has a great deal to learn from the methods of modern science. We need to recover in religion the reverence for truth shown by the scientist, and his humility as he searches for it. We need to recover his readiness to put away preconceived opinions, and what he would dearly like to be true, and to seek the high, white star of truth,

wherever it may lead us. I can't imagine a
scientist making a creed, and rejoicing in it
because it is so many centuries old, and then
making words mean what they don't say,
and giving them private interpretations of
his own in order to provide a spurious
appearance of unity with the thinkers of long
ago. As Froude the historian said, " If
medicine had been regulated three hundred
years ago by Act of Parliament; if there
had been 39 articles of Physic and every
licensed practitioner had been compelled
under pains and penalties to compound his
drugs by the prescriptions of Henry the
Eighth's physician, Dr. Butts, it is easy to
conjecture in what state of health the people
of this country would at present be found."
The spiritual state of our health can be
partly accounted for by similar obscurant-
ism in sincere and progressive religious
thinking. The unintelligent effort has been
made, not to find out the truth, but to
preserve Christianity unchanged. " The
Churches ", said the late Clutton Brock,
" are not taken seriously because they think
officially, because they seem tied by the leg
to certain dogmas, however long their tether

may be. Their apologetics, when most liberal and intelligent, remain apologetics, having for their aim, not the discovery of truth but the proof that there is still some vestige of truth in Christianity." Certain basal facts are true for ever, of course, but the theologian has been more concerned to defend tradition than to discover truth, and the consequence is that in this modern world *he is left hugging words to his heart when the strength of the truth is no longer in them.* He is like a man hungrily trying to buy food in a foreign town with money that belongs to another, unacceptable, coinage.

It is a thousand pities that, because of this preference for tradition, intellectual leadership has now passed from religion to science, and this is all the more regrettable because science, as such, is not concerned with the ethical question as to the use to which scientific discoveries should be put.

Those who desire to find their anchor hold in the strain and stress of life must not cling to tradition unless it also has in it the strength of the truth. Their faith will no doubt be beyond scientific demonstration, but it should not be a wild guess, an undisciplined fancy, but based on rock-like truth. They must be prepared to think, for we are commanded to love the Lord our God with all our *mind*, and Christ criticised religious tradition more severely than He criticised " the world ", and always taught that new light seeks to burst through the chinks of old, musty forms. It is not irreverent to ask questions about the hoariest tradition, for no truth is really of value to us until we see it to be true for ourselves.

The same is true in regard to authority. Authority may be a way of approaching truth. If some distinguished person or group of persons—the saints, for instance— holds certain things as true, it is *primâ facie* evidence that investigation is worth while. But the best minds cannot accept a statement on the authority of another, *and give it power to hold the heart in secure anchorage*, until that gleam of recognition of which I have spoken has given it its surest validity. Even the alleged words of Jesus may reverently be subjected to this test. For instance, it is impossible to believe that Jesus said, " All that ever came before Me are thieves and robbers " (John 10[8]), unless the words can be given another meaning. We reject authority, even that of the Bible —yes, even if we are told Jesus spoke them—because the leap of recognition does not take place. It is just not like Him to say that. We cannot fit it in to our temple of truth. We have such a discriminating inner sense of Truth, such a dependable court of justice in the breast, that we seem to know when we are being misinformed about Jesus. It is because Christ is Himself the Truth within us. Later, we may find that the Greek words mean " political revolutionaries ", not thieves and robbers in our sense. Then we can accept the word. But authority alone does not bring the mind to the place where it can rest—does not, in a word, convince it of truth. Only when truth becomes our own, born again for us in the silence of the deep places of our lives, has it power and strength. The only authority, the only credential truth has is itself. If a scientist tells us that the distance between a certain star and another is ten million miles, most of us accept the statement readily enough, but facts of that kind are not relevant to the living of our lives. What I have written is profoundly true in the realm of the truths by which we live our lives from day to day. Unless we have a peculiar quality of mind—not, I think, to be desired—we cannot accept truth which is relevant to the business of living merely on the authority of another, however impressive that authority may be.

It is very significant here to realise that Jesus spoke with authority. We are told (Mark 12³⁷) that the common people heard Him gladly because He spoke with author-ity, and not as the Scribes. Why, the Scribes were the very people who *had* authority! But when Jesus spoke, the leap of recognition took place. Men knew He was right by that response which the spirit of man makes when it is confronted with what is beautiful and good—and true. He used the only authority truth has— itself. He didn't ask you to believe a thing because some ancient old Rabbi said it was so. He asked you to believe it and live by it because you could see it to be lovely and true. The flash of recognition passed, the response only given to an ultimate, took place.

I exult in the eternal strength of the truth. It will irresistibly emerge. We needn't "tremble for the ark of God". One man believes one thing and one another. Never mind! The truth of both will live. The Christianity we know hasn't a monopoly of all truth. Before Christianity is seen to be the final religion, it must make reverent and glad room for the truth contained in every cult from every ocean and every shore.

> God's gift was that man should conceive of truth
> And yearn to gain it, catching at mistake
> As midway help till he reach fact indeed.[1]

I exult in the fact that nothing can kill the truth, hidden though it may be for a time. Absolute truth we cannot know, or we should be God. When Jesus said, " I am the Truth," He made a claim to divinity. But let us not be afraid. The truth is broad and strong, and God reveals enough Rock for you to get your anchor fixed on.

Men did Christ to death. They thought that was the end. But truth remained to

---

[1] Browning's " A Death in the Desert ".

scourge them with scorpions.   As Masefield
makes the lily-seller say :—

Friend, it is over now, the passion, the sweat, the pains.
Only the truth remains.[1]

In your dark moments look round on a
world swayed by violence.   Add the dark
deeds together—China, Abyssinia, Spain,
Palestine, Czecho-Slovakia, Poland, Norway,
Holland, Belgium, France, Greece. . . .

> Though the cause of Evil prosper,
> Yet 'tis Truth alone is strong,
> Though her portion be the scaffold
> And upon the throne be wrong,
>
> Yet the scaffold sways the future,
> And, behind the dim unknown,
> Standeth God within the shadow,
> Keeping watch above His own.[2]

Andrew Melville has been called " a
Greatheart of the Reformation ".   The Earl
of Morton threatened him with violent
death, but Andrew Melville laughed his
threatening to scorn.   " Tush, tush, my
Lord," he said, in words which every
Scotsman knows, " make these threats to
your courtiers.   It is all one to me whether

[1] Good Friday.
[2] Lowell's " The Present Crisis ".

R

I rot in the air or in the earth. *It is not in your power to hang or exile the truth.*"

Make search, my soul, for truth. Let truth lay hold on thee. Don't try to defend a line that stretches from Genesis to Revelation, and on through all the creeds of men, nor feel that His cause is threatened because a breach in the line is made at the book of Jonah! Oh, how we fight for details, die for a convention, argue passionately for a ritual, scream over unessentials and miss the calm, solid, eternal dignity of TRUTH! Make sure of God, His nature, His power, His purpose, His grace. Whittle down your creed to a few words, if need be, so long as it is *your* creed, and not a mumbo-jumbo of words you took over from some long-dead ancestor. Let your certainty grow slowly if need be, so long as your anchor firmly grips the *truth*. The truth will keep your heart steady in the storm. The truth will make you *free*. Test it and try it for yourself. For Christianity is REAL. It isn't a pretty picture we looked at in childhood. It's as real as the Rock of Gibraltar. You can get to it and test it for yourself. It may not have become real to you yet, any more than Gibraltar was real to the woman in those early days when she made the tea for her parents. But it can become real to you if you take the vessel of faith and launch away and test it and try it out.

Religion may be to you a fog of abstract notions, a shifting sand of ideas about which people quarrel, a mere clash of opinions, a bewildering desert of creeds and rituals and theologies and ordinances. I won't write of these differences now. Some are important. Others are not as important as they seem. But out of them, like Gibraltar out of the sea-mist that sometimes clings to its base, soars the mighty Truth, the solid Rock, the strong thing that is our Refuge and Strength, and about this every denomination agrees; about this all the saints are one, whether Anglo-Catholic or Salvationist, Quaker or Methodist : *Jesus Christ can make all the difference to life*, and that Jesus is alive and available. That is the truth behind the Christian Faith. He can make all the difference : the difference between despair and courage, defeatism and tenacity, depression and an underlying faith in face of the worst, hectic, fevered futility and serenity, self-pity and service to others, the utter depression of sin and the acceptance of forgiveness, a new start and a new power.

If you ask me for evidence, I am only embarrassed, because there is so much from which to choose. A book recently published, called " Under Thirty Speaks for Christ ", is just a fragment of modern evidence from young people of almost every profession, social position and point of view, that they have found the Rock " wherein sure their soul's anchor may remain ". Any *live* Christian, any missionary from the field, would tell you how true it all is. Could faith based in a lie alter the lives of men and women throughout the world for two thousand years ?

Here is just one letter which happened to come my way. A soldier's wife writes :—

" When my husband went into the army at the beginning of the war, I felt too unhappy to care about the future. I was afraid of the responsibility of carrying on the home and bringing up our two young children, but the thing that made me most unhappy was the fear that he would never come back again. I cried myself to sleep at nights, and when things went wrong during the day, as they frequently did, I lost my temper, slapped the children, and blamed Hitler for it all. My letters to my husband did nothing to help him face the difficulties of his new life, and, when he came home for a few hours' leave, my constant dread that it was the last time I should ever see him, created such a feeling in the home that everybody was acutely miserable.

" I tried many times to be different, but always failed. As a last resort I decided to turn to God. These last weeks my only regret has been that I didn't take this step years ago. My husband and I have reached such complete understanding that we can accept the separation willingly and cheerfully. The burden which I found responsibility to be has vanished, and our home is becoming a happier place. Now I don't need to try to be cheerful. I am happy."

Every week I could give you evidence like that. So don't say, " Well, it's not for me." Why not you? You are just being content that the Rock, Christ, should be a picture in your mind. Launch out. Set sail. Go and see for yourself. Try Him! Get your feet on the Rock! Offer yourself to Him. Don't wait to get your intellectual questions answered. Don't wait till the end of the war. Don't wait till you can put yourself into some kind of moral repair. Venture on Christ. Trust Him. Instead of letting your troubles make God seem unreal, let them drive you to Him. Here is a great word of Hudson Taylor : " It doesn't matter how great the pressure is, it only matters where the pressure lies; whether it comes between you and God or whether it presses you near and ever nearer to His heart of love." That love is real.

I'm not going to pretend that to live on that Rock is as easy as catching a liner and waking up one morning to find yourself at Gibraltar. Sometimes the supreme experience seems to come of itself. Winifred Holtby had been told by a specialist that

she might not have more than two years to
live, and her mind—vigorously alive in her
slow, impaired body—rebelled bitterly
against her fate, for she was only thirty-
three. She was standing in a farmyard by
a trough of water which was frozen, and
some young lambs were vainly trying to
drink. She broke the ice for them with
her stick, and as she did so she heard a
voice within her saying, " Having nothing,
yet possessing all things." It was so dis-
tinct that she looked round, startled, but
she was alone with the lambs on the top
of the hill. Suddenly, in a flash, the grief,
the bitterness, the sense of frustration disappeared; all desire to possess power and
glory for herself vanished away and never
came back. She walked down the hill with
a feeling of exhilaration instead of the despair with which she had ascended. She
only told her friends of this experience three
months before her death. The moment of
" conversion " on the hill, she said, was
the supreme spiritual experience of her
life.

Usually it means constantly offering ourselves, going back, again and again, for

pardon and renewal. But it is worth it, for *when we have stopped counting on all other so-called securities*, like health, business, prosperity, home-happiness, the love of dear ones; when we realise that, however desirable and however much they are God's desire for us, they may, in the present chaos, disappear, then a strange new peace invades us. We have found the ultimate harbour of the spirit in which nothing can harm us any more. It is when we have faced having nothing that we possess all things, for we realise that He is ours, and that He is all that matters, that all things are in His hands, that nothing can touch our security, for it is Himself, and that our dear ones—whom He loves better than we do—are in His hands too, and that, whatever happens, God remains the firm, immovable Rock, the Omnipotent Lover, the Friend whose friendship nothing can destroy. And because He lives and reigns, all that is of Him, including ourselves, is safe. Nothing can ultimately defeat His purpose or prevent Him from bringing us at last into the haven where He wants us to be.

Though waves and storms go o'er my head,
Though strength, and health, and friends be gone,
Though joys be withered all and dead,
Though every comfort be withdrawn,
On this my steadfast soul relies—
Father, Thy mercy never dies !

Fixed on this ground will I remain,
Though my heart fail and flesh decay :
This anchor shall my soul sustain,
When earth's foundations melt away :
Mercy's full power I then shall prove,
Loved with an everlasting love.[1]

It is the solid Truth that Christ lived. It is the solid Truth that He lives. It is the solid Truth that millions have found in Him their all. Their testimony is that when they found Him nothing else vitally mattered. Is not Truth an ally of Faith? May we not find Him too? By faith we may, whatever the world may say or do. "This is the victory that overcometh the world, even our faith."

[1] Rothe, translated by John Wesley.

PART III
FAITH'S FORWARD LOOK

CHAPTER FOURTEEN

FAITH IN THE CHURCH ETERNAL

WHEN WE WERE CHILDREN, IF SOMEONE HAD asked us what we meant by " the Church ", we should probably have told them about the building at the corner of the road in which we worshipped with our parents. When we got older we should have defined the word in terms of our denomination. Later still, our views would have widened to include all men and women everywhere, of all races and creeds, who loved and believed in the Lord Jesus Christ and tried to follow His way of life.

That last would pass as a description of the Church on earth, but it is of very great importance, in my judgment, to realise that even that wide vision is not big enough.

The Church is not something that began on earth and then, as men and women passed away, existed also in heaven. *The Church came down out of heaven from God.* That sentence seems to me the most important thing that can be said about the

Church, though it sounds strange and even repellent to modern ears which dislike any reference to the supernatural.

In St. John's lovely vision in the last book in the Bible we find that the Holy City has no temple. The Community and the Church are one and the same. He saw " no temple therein " [1] but he saw the Holy City "coming down out of Heaven from God ".[2]

The Church *on earth* began when Jesus, in St. Mark's lovely phrase, chose twelve men " that they might be with Him ", and every denomination has developed from that fellowship. But there is no denomination that is not, in a sense, a mere shadow— perhaps a caricature—of that beauteous, holy and perfect fellowship in the unseen and eternal world which existed before this little insignificant planet began its course, and which will go on when the earth hangs like the moon, a frozen planet in the sky, or is burnt up in the sun which gave it birth.

We realise this awesome truth in the Communion Service when we adore God, saying, " Therefore with angels and arch-angels and all the company of heaven, we laud and magnify Thy glorious name,

[1] Rev. 21[22].   [2] Rev. 21[10].

evermore praising Thee and saying, ' Holy, holy, holy, Lord God of Hosts. Heaven and earth are full of Thy glory. Glory be to Thee, O Lord Most High.' "

If I could make every Church member see that vision of the Church, he would say in a hushed voice to himself, " I, even I, am allowed to belong to that august communion." To see such a vision is to realise that being a Church member is the most wonderful privilege life can offer, and one of the most powerful ways of maintaining faith during days of stress and storm.

Illustrations are not easy to find, but there is one to hand as we think of the life of Christ. It was not the life of a Man who became so good that He was dubbed divine. Achievement had its necessary part in His nature, but we most truly understand the Incarnation, not when we regard it as a climbing up into divinity, on the part of a man, but as a coming down of God from the eternal, unseen world and expressing Himself in the life of man. Jesus is not man become God, but God become Man, and His life was a reflection, a shadow, a translation into humanity, of the life of God. In the same way the Church is not something born on earth which grew to divine proportions and significance, but a translation into terms of space and time of the divine community eternally existent in Heaven. You belong to *that*!

Therefore, as I think today with gratitude of any of the Churches which mean much to me, the Church of my youth which meant so much to me, and the Churches of which I have been the minister, I see them stretching their hands outward and touching all communions of Christians, whatever their denominational label, in all lands, on all shores, under all skies. I see them stretching their hands forward to hand on the torch to those who come after, until, perhaps, they cover the earth. I see them stretching their hands backward, their hands touching those of the generation before us, and so back and back until the last man slips his hand into the hand of Christ. But most importantly I see the hands of these tiny branches of the Church stretched upward to link not only with those who have gone into the unseen, but with angels and archangels and all the company of heaven who worship God with unveiled faces in the Eternal Beauty.

My faith in the Church is not faith in the drab and unbeautiful building at the corner of the road, where Mrs. Smith won't speak to Mrs. Brown because she was snubbed twenty years ago, or where Mr. Jones resigns once a month in the hope of getting his own way and blackmailing his minister, or where Mr. Robinson sings lustily that he is "washed in the blood of the Lamb," but would not tolerate a stranger in his pew and has not paid his milkman's bill, where Mrs. Jenkins attends every service and every meeting and "adores the dear vicar," but makes a hell of her own home by her temper, tears and tantrums, or where committees wrangle and fight about trivialities, gossip behind one another's backs, and show less goodwill and good-fellowship than one finds in a golf-club committee or in an Army Mess where nothing is professed save decency and gentlemanliness. It is not easy to keep a vision bright and faith strong in a Church where the minister is submerged in such an endless effort to raise money that the *raison d'être* of the Church is lost sight of completely, where bazaars, whist-drives, dances and dramatic performances are given much more prominence than changing men's

s

lives, and where every new enterprise—
floated usually on tea—aims at money
rather than men.

From the conception of the Church Eternal many truths about the Church emerge,
with which there is no space to deal adequately, though I will state some of them :—

(1) How foolish it is for critics to speak
of the Church failing ! Whenever men
really grasp an eternal idea they never let it
go.   They express it in various ways, and
the *expressions* are imperfect, and sometimes fail.   The idea may be lost sight of for
years, but, once grasped, it leaps out again
in this form and in that, and never dis-
appears.   The idea of the brotherhood of
man has been seen.   It is in danger of being
lost sight of, and one form of it—the League
of Nations—broke, but already men dream
of another, Federal Union; and the *idea*
will never die.   The same is true of the
Church.   I hope its denominations *will*
fail, that their purpose will exhaust their
raison d'être, but the *idea* will never die,
for it is eternal.   All its expressions may
break down, but it is part of eternal truth,
and we shall be driven to accept it and live
by it.   No foolishness or devilry of ours can

make or destroy truth. Every denomination may be seen to be a passing phase, but the eternal fellowship of God with men is part of invulnerable truth. The Church is eternal. On this truth alone faith in the future is justified.

(2) How foolish it is to make the Church's threshold low and beseech men to cross it by offering them inducements ! " Come and join our Church—you will find billiards, dances, whist drives, tennis parties. . . ." These things may have a place as expressions of the fellowship of men and women *already committed to God* themselves and desirous of showing forth His power and love, but the inducements and " stunts ", should they fill our churches, would do only the greater harm, for people are made immeasurably to misunderstand the whole nature of the Church by such methods. Further, you get the best human response not by making entrance easy, but difficult ; not by inducements, but by the call to sacrificial service. How utterly degrading it is for the Church to have people in it who come because they thus do a favour to those who invite them, or come for what they can get in terms of a cheap social club !

We should follow Jesus more closely if we tried to keep people out until they saw membership as the greatest privilege of their lives and a commitment that might cost them all they had. The curse of the Church at present is that it is cluttered up with well-meaning, anæmic people who have never taken Christ seriously, and do not even intend to do so, and who, through years of church-going, have developed such a thick armour against the shafts of Jesus that His most searching and scathing words neither challenge nor touch them. The trouble is that, not entering His Kingdom themselves, they stop others, for assuredly no one wants to be like *them*. There is no rich quality about their lives or their mastery of its problems that makes others long to share their secret. Actually the Churches can count on very few of its members really showing forth the way of Christ in the world. A high percentage of its members are not changed themselves. Therefore, of course, they have no burning message or witness for others. Many are willing to work in order to " fill the church ". They have no vision of what the Church exists to offer to those who fill it. They don't see that they are bluffing themselves, and trying to bluff God and evade His challenge to them, by pressing others to accept what they have refused. "Come and be like us," they cry. But the man in the street says in his heart, "From ever being like you may your God deliver me."

(3) A third point I would make is that while there are many people in the Church who ought to be out, there are many out who ought to be in. Too many people stand aloof from the Church *because* it does not express their ideal of what the Church should be. May I say to them very bluntly : "You are standing outside the Church to criticise it and call it names, obtaining thus a lovely dug-out in which you hide from God, obtaining thus a grand excuse for spiritual slackness, and deceiving yourself that the Church is such a poor thing that it is unworthy of your support. I wonder when it will have progressed far enough for *you* to condescend to belong to it? Is there not a far finer attitude? To feel acutely and sensitively all the failings of the Church, but to stand in with her and try to make her what she ought to be, to make the translation into terms of human fellowship of a

Divine idea a better translation by *your* devotion and *your* service."

The Taj Mahal is a translation into white marble of the idea of a husband about his beloved wife who had passed on. It took twenty thousand workmen twenty years to build it up, and cost over three million pounds. A bomb could smash it in a moment, and, since the mind that conceived it cannot again work it out, the destruction would be complete. Which is the nobler, to build and rebuild and build better, or to pull down and try to smash with no thought of helping God to build better?

Those who stand outside the Church because of her defects forget that their logic is sadly at fault. Who would fight for England because the War Office and the multiple organisations of war were perfect? We fight that a dream may come true, and the faultier the organisation the harder we must fight. "I don't go to church," said a man recently, "I don't like this and I don't like that, and I don't get anything out of it." Can you imagine an Englishman saying, "I won't fight for England and liberty. I don't like the way the food is served and I don't like the language of the

Sergeant-Major "? He who goes into war to get something out of it must be half-witted. You fight and serve to put something into it, to make a dream come true.

One day it may be true to sing, " Like a mighty army, moves the Church of God." One would not feel that denominational barriers were such terrible wounds in the body of Christ if all Church members were united in an unbroken front against evil and united in one desire and in one loyalty to one Lord. Then the denominations might function as various regiments in one army, or as the separate fingers of one right hand, closed into a fist against wrong. Do try to see beyond tea-meetings and quarrelling committees and antique phrases and bewildering ritual and complicated creeds and ornate ceremonies and tiresome, fussy people who get upset if you sit in their pew and trample on their opinions, or don't give them what they consider to be their just mead of praise. Try to see the Galilean standing on the beach, with the blue sky above Him and the green hills behind Him, the waves rippling to His feet, with the sorrows of the whole world on His spirit, but with the unquenchable joy of God in His eyes, calling to men, to you and to me, to show the world a new way of life and reveal the beauty and glory of God. For *that* is what the Church exists to offer—to offer men Christ, to bring them into the eternal fellowship of this holy, supernatural, august thing which men called the " body of Christ ".

I could fill many pages with a list of the splendid things of which the Church of Christ has been the initiator and the sustaining power. I have seen the Indian village untouched by Christian influences, and I know some of the things the Church has done. It has lifted manhood, redeemed womanhood, shown how precious is the life of the child. It has a thousand tasks to do still, but don't forget that in spite of a record anyone can criticise, no other organisation has come near it in lifting human life and in carrying its enheartening message to every nation.

Real progress has more truly come through the influence of the Christian Church than through any other organisation in the world.

The Christian Church is the only international organisation in the world, and, in my view, the only hope of redeeming the world. If cleverness, or diplomacy, or force, or scientific invention, or talking could save the world, it would be saved by now. We need God, *coming down* into human life and doing in the world and for it what it will never do for itself and what the Church, God's chosen instrument, alone can do.

Many are in the mood to scoff at such a claim. I pass on to them the word of a Hyde park orator, only wishing that my own brain worked so quickly. A man in the crowd shouted, " Christianity has been in the world for two thousand years, and look at the state of the world." " Yes," replied the orator without a second's hesitation, " and water has been in the world for two million years, and look at the state of your face." Salvation is available. It must be applied. A new way of life is offered. It must be tried out.

In the first quarter of the first century, words were spoken and a life lived in Galilee which still fascinate and challenge and attract the world. When men criticise the Church, I feel it is largely because we who are in it are so unlike Him. In it or out of it, we are all to some extent responsible for the awful mess the world is in.

It is not for the Church to talk of politics or sociology or economy, but to offer men Christ, in surrender to Whom their lives can be changed and sent out to interpret in politics and commerce and reform those truths which He will make clear to them if they will open their hearts to His Spirit.

Frankly, can you see any hope anywhere else ? We are cleverer than men have ever been. We want peace—if it be honourable and just—more than men have ever wanted it. Never was war begun with greater reluctance and waged with less hate. But all our plans for a new world fail because we haven't the dynamic, infectious, unselfish good-will which only comes from a surrender to God, and the subsequent control by God, of every part of our life together.

Our eyes are on Hitler, our hopes are that revolution may happen in Germany, that Russia may save us, that America will help us or that something else may happen. But apart from the unfaith of scaling down our expectancy to purely human guesses, as though God were not actively at work and able to alter the whole situation and end the war, can we really do anything better for the peace of the world than become the kind of people —utterly dedicated—whom God can most fully use? That, it seems to me, is the Church's message. " Follow Me " was the word of Christ. My faith is in Him. The Church on earth in all its branches is the organised fellowship of those who are trying to follow Him. Therefore I have faith in that fellowship.

There is a familiar legend that when Jesus returned to Heaven, His work on earth finished, the angel Gabriel met Him and asked what plans his Lord had made to make sure that His work was carried on. " I have given the message to Peter and John, to Mary and Martha," Jesus answered. " They will tell others, and thus the message will spread." " But supposing," said the angel Gabriel, " that the fishermen are too busy with their fishing and the women with their housework, so that they forget to tell their friends, or the friends forget to pass the message on. What other plans hast thou made, Lord? "

Jesus paused and smiled a wonderful smile. " I have no other plans," He answered quietly,—" I am counting on them."

CHAPTER FIFTEEN

FAITH IN THE CHURCH OF TOMORROW[1]

I BELIEVE THAT THE GREATEST TROUBLE IN
the churches today is that a high percentage
of our people—numbers are dangerous and
inaccurate, but perhaps nearly ninety per
cent.—are spiritually without the vital
experience of Christ which is gloriously
offered in the New Testament. They are
familiar with what Christ says, in some
cases they are attracted, hungry and wistful,
but not surrendered, not commited, not won.
Therefore in their lives the promises are not
fulfilled and the fruits are not obvious.
Their Christianity, in fact, is not the real
thing, but a spurious substitute. It is not
alive. Based not on surrender, but on com-
promise, it is a conventional and poor copy
of the real thing. In their hearts they know

[1] Part of this chapter appeared in substance as a
Foreword to the volume called " The Finger of God "
by Mr. Frank Raynor (Group Publications, Ltd.).

it is a sham, for there is no power in it. In their hearts they know it is a lie—such a poor lie that it has not even convinced *them*. In their hearts they know it is a fake, and the pathetic illusion of reality is kept up by attendance at services, a dangerous anæsthetic; or by hectic service on this committee and that, a dangerous drug; or by passionate discussion of this problem or that, so often a deep dug-out. So many church-going people, many of them hereditarily so, are strangers to a living, vital relation with a Christ who is changing them and directing them daily and who through them is changing others; strangers to a sense of forgiveness and harmony in which the soul can look up to God and truly say, " There is nothing between us "; strangers to a sense of power to do things previously impossible, especially power over sin; strangers to a sense of joy which is independent of money, health, success and high spirits; strangers to a sense of peace independent of whether the diary is full or empty, whether business is flourishing or failing, whether the country is at war or not; strangers to a sense of love for others which includes the hostile, the critical, and those who are more successful than themselves. These things—the marks of an authentic experience of Christ—which are all offered are not possessed, and many " church people " know they do not possess them. Unwilling utterly to surrender, they make do with a religion which is not Christianity at all, which uses the jargon without the reality, the form without the fire.

Not Christianity at all? No, surely an enemy of Christianity more insidious than, say, Communism. In Palestine in the first century, the greatest enemy of Christianity was religion. My opinion is that in Britain in the twentieth century one of the greatest enemies of Christianity is a religion *called* Christianity which is a pale imitation of the real thing. In the first century the Christian was the best advertisement of the new faith. His joy, his sense of power over sin, his radiant happiness, his serene trust, just *made* people want what he had got. Christianity spread like some glorious infection against which even strongholds of paganism were not immune. Can we honestly say this of most church-going people today? In many cases church-goers are definitely putting people off. They don't leave them untouched. They leave them prejudiced. They are going about with a spurious thing they think is religion. It may be, but it is not the Christian religion. It is too smug, too complacent, too compromising, too comfortable, too unadventurous, too pedestrian for the real thing.

I shall be told I am exaggerating. Very well, let the reader get pencil and paper and write down the names of the people in his church who, *from their own experience*—not by lending a book, or taking to hear a preacher—could lead another soul to Christ. Let us face some personal questions. Have we got an experience of Christ that we long to pass on? Have we got an experience of Christ that makes others long to have what we've got? If another asked us how he might find the transforming experience which is the central thing in Christianity, would we know what to do with him? If all the Christians in the early Church had been like us, how far would Christianity have spread? Are we displaying a quality of life that makes us good advertisements of Christianity? Do our lives really reveal the glory of Christ's power and loveliness? Let

us sit down, and quietly and slowly ask
ourselves each of those questions !

The early Christians simply astonished
the pagan. He sat up and said to himself,
" These people have no money, no prestige,
no special culture, but they've got what all
the world is looking for, the secret of the mastery of the art of living." They were intoxicated with the wine of a new life. They
couldn't keep it to themselves. Simply and
directly they could communicate this tremendous experience to another. The mighty
parables of Jesus had come true. It was like
finding a pearl worth losing everything to
gain; like finding a treasure in a field that
made you rich for life; like being at home
again after a long experience of swine-
troughs. The dramatic metaphors of Paul
were sober facts. One passed from darkness to light, slavery to sonship, captivity
to liberty, death to life. Say it, you who
have been lost in a jungle at midnight, who
spent weary years a prisoner of war, who
stood by the grave of a lover. Darkness
to light, captivity to liberty, death to life.
Does it honestly mean this to us? Have
we got the real thing at all? It is incredible
that anyone should possess the real thing

and be able to keep it as dark as we keep our religion. If we knew a cure for cancer, should we babble about our reticence and our reserve? Having established fellowship, should we not tell the good news to those in the toils of the disease? The man who says he is a Christian says by that fact that he knows a power that can triumph over sin, offer forgiveness, bring peace to the soul, joy to the heart, love to the spirit. If he says he has been a Christian for twenty years and has never lifted pen or voice or finger to bring another to Christ, he is like a man walking about a plague-cursed island keeping what he *says* is a cure in his pocket. There are only three explanations. He doesn't believe in it himself. He has never tried it. He hasn't got the real thing.[1]

Where is the ecstasy that used to sing :—

" My heart it doth dance at the sound of His name " ?

Where is the longing to pass on what the

[1] In likening sin to disease it is, in my view, very important to distinguish between sin and moral disease. Sin needs forgiveness and the new start. Moral disease needs treatment, spiritual or psychological, or, ideally, both.

T

soul had found such as is expressed in Charles Wesley's hymn beginning :—

> " O for a thousand tongues to sing
>   My great Redeemer's praise ! " ?

John Freeman in his haunting poem " The Alde " gives us a picture of that river running quietly through the familiar lands, so near to the sea. The sea-birds wheel over it. It hears the waves beating on the shore,

> But the uncertain river, though it crave
>   The sea, knows not the sea.

Then the salt wind, the wild waters, the " new troubling tide of eager waves that pour around and over ", the fresh water changed to salt. The river finds that for which every river was born, the sea.

What a parable of the conventional " Christian " life ! It runs so quietly, and not without beauty, through the familiar lands. It came to me as a shock recently to realise that there is not a single theme on religion about which I can preach but my hearers could say of it, " Yes, we know." " Forgiveness ? " " Oh, yes ", they say at the end of their prayers—nicely tucked in so that sin won't be looked at too closely—

" And this we ask with the forgiveness of all our sins." " Providence? " " Oh yes, in a general way." " Guidance? " " Yes, not many personal illustrations of it, perhaps." " Atonement? " " Oh yes, they believe that Christ died to take away the sins of the world. He hasn't dealt with theirs yet, but they go on telling themselves that the Atonement must mean something." Oh, these familiar meadows in which the river of spiritual life seems to meander on and on and on, never finding the Sea ! We ministers go on preaching and talking and discussing and arguing. Some of our people know the answer to every religious question we can ask except one, and that is the most important, " What must I do to be saved? "

And for so many it means just surrendering at one point where there is an obstacle which stands between us and Christ, some love of self, a self at the centre of our world, some secret sin to which we cling even while we pray for deliverance, some fear of what people might say or think or do, some lingering suspicion that after all the worldling may have a better time of it, some shirking of the discipline of keeping in God's world, a discipline which we gave up,

making our " Christian experience " only a
beautiful memory of something that happened long ago instead of a present power,
some refusal to forgive another or lower our
pride or apologise to one we wronged, some
intellectual difficulty under which we hide
from a Christ who asks first, not for a clear
head and a credal system, but an utter
loyalty of heart, some service which we
offer Christ, hoping to bluff Him; hoping
He will accept our service instead of asking
for ourselves, like a child who has grieved
his mother and proffers to run an errand in
order to try to get things right which can
only be put right when he is in her arms
craving forgiveness. With these things we
block ourselves off from Him, breaking His
heart, denying ourselves the greatest thing
life offers, and spoiling the witness of the
Church in the world. We are like those of
whom Miss Underhill writes, " They have
deserted Christ and entered His service
instead."

I have failed, and do fail, at so many
points in my own ministry that I want to
make it very clear that I am not suggesting
that in the Church of the future we shall all
use similar methods. I do not mean to

imply any disrespect of men who spend much time on organisation, committee and institutional work. I marvel at many of the latter, and wonder how they keep their souls alive. Many of my friends have accepted offices in the ministry which compel them to do more than " save souls ". I certainly do not mean to imply that we should go about " saving souls " as the blatant manner of some is. It is a kind of moral burglary to break into a man's soul before fellowship is established and his heart welcomes us as guests. People who prattle much about " the blood " and ask the man next them on the tram if he is " saved " usually deserve more than they get. But we all, I maintain, ought to be ready and able and eager, *out of our own experience* to lead others to Him. And if our experience of Him dwindles or dies, our *raison d'être* as ministers goes with it. We are not even vital Christians.

We shall differ in our approach, but we shall not differ in our aim. I should be glad to think that at last we had enough courage to change our methods. Surely, the Church of the future will do so. No doctor in London is using only the methods which were used fifty years ago. Are we quite sure that religion can best be " put over " by two services each Sunday, always proceeding in the same way—Hymn, Prayer, Hymn, Lesson, etc.? In olden days the " parson " got that nickname because he was the only " *persona* ", the only educated person, the only means of getting religious information reliably, the only available medium of the living truth of Christ interpreted to meet men's needs. But now, with better education, access to books, wireless and so on, it is not to be supposed that young people will worship God in the old way if they have to listen to one whom they cannot challenge, especially if, as is often the case, the education of the pulpit is not higher than that of the pew, or if, as is frequently the case, the message is offered with such misgiving that it is easier to pick up the misgiving than the message, the latter being covered over with a dullness which dims all its glory and effectively robs it of its power to challenge and inspire. Sometimes when I have seen (or been) a dispirited minister in a great barn of a chapel holding a thousand and containing fifty or sixty depressed looking people, I have wished we could have broken up into three or four groups, prayed together, and asked ourselves and God what was *His* way of dealing with the situation. All the blame cannot be put on people for being indifferent, or on the parson for being dull. Where religion is shown to be thrilling, alive, radiant, dynamic, and of supreme importance and urgent consideration by a minister who himself has never ceased to wonder at the glory and splendour of God's grace, then people come and come again, and most problems get solved. One of the most depressing things in the world is the spectacle of a dead church and a dead minister going through depressing forms, Sunday by Sunday, in an unexpectant, dreary atmosphere, dolefully singing hymns written in moments of white-hot passion, listening sleepily and unexpectantly to the words of Christ which have driven others out to risk all in adventure for His sake, and then going home from chapel to eat Yorkshire pudding and roast beef, followed by a deeper somnolence than was possible even in the sermon, a somnolence sweetened by a feeling of immense superiority to those who saw the gay, royal, glorious Christ on the moors in a

solitary walk, but who just cannot bear the
degradation and ugliness of some services,
which, to them, are as indecent as tying dirty
corsets round the Venus de Milo, making
coarse and vulgar an expression of the joy
and beauty of God.

Many ministers felt the challenge of
the various group movements. They asked
themselves before God what they were
going to do about it. After a re-dedication
of themselves they went out in the spirit of a
fine old Gaelic saying which has been with
me much of late, " I, too, will turn my face
to the wind and cast my handful of seed on
high." Many such men found, to their utter
amazement, that God gave them a harvest
at once. But in a few cases men had been
making excuses. They had been telling
themselves that they were not evangelists,
that they were doing other, but not less important, work, that they did not believe in
evangelistic methods and so forth, when the
real truth was that they had themselves
ceased to have a vital experience of Christ
worth handing on. Many, quite honestly,
had ceased to pray, save in a merely per-
functory way or as their work demanded.
Some had never led a single soul to Christ.

Some would not have known what to do with a seeking and penitent soul. Some offered a dull sermon every Sunday with, at heart, a thinly veiled hostility against their people who seemed so apathetic and so critical and small-minded. Some, for many weary months, had been rebuking people for not wanting what they themselves had not got. They became the kind of official clergy which the man in the street so naturally hates and distrusts; a mass of repressions, formalities, inhibitions and conventions, attending innumerable committees, producing even in themselves the sense that they were " terribly busy " when in reality they were busy with the things which matter second, not the things we were ordained to do. Now, some who were challenged and who responded have got over it. They have slipped back into the old groove, and once more it is becoming a grave. The number of " groupers " who have got over it and now dislike being thus labelled is significant.

But God can change all that and has done so for hundreds. Let those same ministers make time each day to pray and listen, to tackle difficult books, to make new sermons

—best of all, to win others to Christ. When pride has gone, a new wondering radiance will shine even in their faces. A love for others will stream from them. Jealousy and indolence, self-deception and excuse will be put away.

What a vital, dynamic, powerful thing the Church of the future could be if all who " call themselves Christians " would, as it were, draw a line and forget the past and start again with a new act of self-dedication ! The Church then could definitely mould the new age.

When ministers and people begin to live lives which are daily surrendered, new chapters in the book of Acts come to be written; the power of Christ's converting grace is newly released, and men know that Christ is indeed the Saviour of the World. Missionary enthusiasm is no longer an attempt to bluff God and ourselves by paying for others to be offered what we ourselves have never really received. And all our hectic committee work and church meetings will be conducted in a new atmosphere because the business side of the Church's life will be seen to be the expression of a precious relationship with Christ, not the evasion of it under the smoke-screen of much activity directed towards bringing in a fictitious Kingdom of God falsely supposed to be brought in by external propaganda. The Kingdom of God is within us. Nothing matters in the world so much as that our hearts should be His, our surrender complete, our dedication fresh every morning. Nothing matters so much as that without delay, in deep penitence, at His feet, we should exchange our dreary, sham religion for the real thing.

The glorious truth remains that revival is possible and that soon it may be here. Men are, at any rate, sick to death of most promised ways which are alleged to lead to a new world. Let us all be in this thing. Either the tides of the Spirit will rush through the present channels of the Church, cleansing, refreshing and bringing new life, or else they will leave it still and stagnant, like some old disused backwater which the rushing waters pass by. The Kingdom of Christ on earth may be coming either through, or in spite of, the Church as now organised. And if the latter, then what is now called the Church will cease to be THE Church. For that eternal reality is not a man-made thing of form or convention. It only exists where the Spirit of Jesus is alive, active and communicable. I believe in the Church of Tomorrow; I am quite sure God has not finished with us yet.

On the doors of our churches I hear the insistent knock of Christ, the Disturber of our peace. But the peace He disturbs is that of a smug, complacent, compromising, insincere, unreal, conventional sham; a bastard, spurious substitute for that glorious thing alone worthy to be called by His name, that breaks down pride and sends men out to change the world.

Therefore He goes on knocking. Oh, my soul, rise up and let Him in! The world needs Him desperately. Only His spirit can purify it. Only His body can redeem it. The Church which is His body!

CHAPTER SIXTEEN

FAITH IN THE NEW WORLD

AT THE CITY TEMPLE WE HAVE A FELLOWSHIP of young people which, before the war, numbered close on four hundred. We meet on Friday evenings to discuss those problems which press upon the minds of youth and which get in the way of the soul's true health. The aim of every meeting is to begin for some, and deepen for us all, that personal communion of the soul with God in Christ which is the heart of the Christian religion. Sometimes the question before us—of which due notice has always been given—is devotional. Here is an example : When you pray, " Be with me, Lord, today ", what do you really expect to happen ? Does it happen ? If not, why not ?

Sometimes the question is theological. We recently spent six weeks on the question, " How can the death of Christ two thousand years ago have relevance to our lives today ? "

Frequently our question deals with the

opposition which young people meet with
in every walk of life as soon as their com-
panions learn that they are " religious ".

Difficult texts in the Bible and the
questions of Biblical interpretation and
inspiration have given us many a profitable
evening.

Our plan is to begin with silence and a
short prayer. Then I open the subject up
very briefly and suggest on what lines our
discussion might move. Then we break
up into groups. We have had seventeen
groups with twenty in a group, and with
visitors attending most groups also. Each
group has its leader and deputy-leader,
its scribe and deputy scribe. The leader
seeks to keep folk to the point without being
" bossy " and doing all the talking. A
shy rather than a talkative person makes the
best type of leader. The scribe does *not*
report what each person says, but reports
briefly the findings of the group, and
particularly any question which the group
would like to have talked out in the open
conference which follows.

Then the fun begins. After the scribes
have reported, the meeting is open for
anyone to speak. There is no hesitation.

The whole meeting aims at being as informal as a group of friends round the fire. Anyone can say anything, but cranks may not speak more than three times !

I want the City Temple pulpit to be free from the charge that it is a coward's castle. So anything I have said there can be challenged on a Friday evening.

I have gone into some detail about the " Friday Fellowship ", in the hope that other churches might try the experiment. In my ministries both in Leeds and London such a fellowship has been spiritually the strongest thing in our Church life. I have been very fortunate in my churches, for the folk who do not even wish to put first things first have always been a very small and unimportant minority amongst the real workers,[1] a minority always growing smaller as young people who are keen on *the real thing* join the Church. A church without *spiritual* fellowship is no church at all, and no amount of socials, concerts, and bazaars

---

[1] I do not allow anyone to hold office in any branch of the Church's life who is not a member of the Church, publicly received at a Communion Service. Everyone who is so received is previously carefully examined as to his motives and sincerity.

and whist-drives can make up for the loss. Here is the Methodist Class Meeting reborn, for here are seventeen class meetings functioning at one time.

I cannot tell how much I have gained personally from being present. It helps me to keep my finger on the pulse of youth's ideas and aspirations. Particularly is this true in regard to what youth wants to see in the new world. The " Social Conscience " of youth is indeed a thing for which to thank God.

Recently I asked a member of this fellowship who represents the thoughts of many, to write down for me all that he would like to see in the new world. I print what he sent me without comment, almost as it was written, save that I have omitted some paragraphs headed " Political ".

INTERNATIONAL.

(1) Abolishment of national sovereignty and the establishment of a federated Government in Europe which should control (a) Defence—merely a police-force composed of volunteers from all countries in the federation, (b) migration, (c) communi-

cations, (*d*) currency, (*e*) trade, (*f*) colonies, etc.

(2) All tariffs, passports and national barriers to be discarded, so that the people of all nations are free to travel where they want, and in this way would feel (after a few generations) that they belong as much to one country as another.

(3) The duty primarily of this Government would be to break the financial ring that now allows one section of the world to starve while food rots in another in order that the price may be kept up.

NATIONAL.

Employment and Labour.

(1) State ownership of all public interests and natural resources—*e.g.*, railways, mines, radium, etc.

(2) A five-day week and an eight-hour day for all workers. Unemployment insurance to cover all classes of worker.

(3) Retiring age to be fixed at 60 years. The old age pension to be such that people can live on it without anxiety.

(4) Two weeks' holiday with pay for all workers—holiday homes to be provided for those who wish to go away.

U

Leisure.

(1) Instructions in schools on the use of leisure.

(2) Formations of clubs, etc., for men to have an opportunity to cultivate hobbies.

(3) Free national theatres for showing good plays and films and giving good concerts, so that the workers may hear good music, etc., in their free time.

(4) Large sections of the country to be open to the public and cheap travelling facilities made available.

(5) Machinery should become the slave of man, not man the slave of the machine. In this way working hours could be greatly reduced and working men could have an opportunity of seeing their own families.

Housing.

(1) Condemned property to be demolished *at once*, and the country to be put to more use—*e.g.*, factories and industries opened in less densely populated areas, as is being done in London.

(2) Houses and flats built for the workers with necessary comforts—*e.g.*, lifts and hot water, so that women don't have to

drag or carry three tired toddlers up 144 stairs after a busy day's work !

(3) Rents to be standardised and to be under the local authorities, and no large blocks of flats to be privately owned.

Public Health.

(1) Health Insurance to cover wife and children as well as the wage-earner.

(2) Sick benefit to be equivalent to average wage, and not need supplementing by application to the relieving officer.

(3) All hospitals to be State financed, and not dependent on charity. Many more to be built, so that workers do not have to wait in suspense for a year or more to have an operation, as is sometimes the case.

(4) Convalescent homes to be provided for after-care treatment.

(5) Five million pounds to be allowed a year for medical research, and more advanced if it can be proved that it is needed.

(6) Compulsory immunisation of all children against diphtheria and scarlet-fever where considered necessary.

(7) Sterilisation of mentally unfit people.

(8) Voluntary euthanasia. In cases of incurable painful disease euthanasia to be

adopted under certain safeguarding conditions.

(9) The use of contraceptives to be taught to all married women, and sterilisation to be available after the birth of the fifth child.

(10) Medical services to be free and available to all.

(11) The supply of milk to be on the same basis as water and electric light—to be supplied to everyone in the country at a small flat rate.

(12) Mental hospitals to be improved, and psychological treatment and psychiatric prevention treatment to be available at far more centres.

(13) All expectant mothers to have an opportunity to rest one month before and one month after confinement. Maternity benefit to be raised.

Incomes and Wages, etc.

(1) All members of the community to have the right and opportunity to earn a living wage.

(2) Revision of income tax to prevent excessive wealth and excessive poverty.

(3) Restriction of inheritable money and

land. Opportunity provided for collective farming.

[Here follow some political suggestions which I do not think are worth printing. My correspondent wants the House of Lords to be abolished, the salaries of Cabinet Ministers reduced, a reduction in allowances to the Royal Family and the adoption of Proportional Representation.] He then writes—

A young people's parliament to be formed of various representatives under thirty years of age. They should be allowed to consider every vital issue before it becomes law—*e.g.*, declaration of war, conscription, etc.

Titles to be given only to those who earned recognition for valuable service to humanity. No titles to be inherited.

Education.

(1) School-leaving age to be raised to 16 years.

(2) Elementary-school education to be improved, so that the average child when he leaves school can speak two languages besides his own, write legibly and have a knowledge of the rest of the world.

(3) Less intelligent children to be taught trades, housekeeping, etc., so they are not a liability when they leave school. The present scheme of interviewing children of school-leaving age with a view to their future should become a State function with the interests of the child, not the employer at heart.

Civic Laws.

(1) Death sentence and all forms of corporal punishment to be abolished.

(2) New prisons built and the psychological aspect given far more consideration.

(3) After-care for prisoners to be a State responsibility, and not a patronising charity.

(4) No person to be imprisoned indefinitely without trial, whether in peace or war.

(5) Magistrates, etc., to be chosen for ability, and not because of social standing. To retire at sixty years.

Unemployment.

As there were two million unemployed before the war, there will probably be many more after it. To those must be added the thousands of men, women and children who

have been disabled, partially or wholly
through air raids. The latter must be free
from anxiety and provided for at all costs.
The former is a problem that has been
allowed to lapse for too long. But as there
is the work—roads, hospitals, slum clear-
ance, etc.—and this war has proved that the
money can be found, the problem should
solve itself if the Government wanted it
solved.

. . . . . .

My friend puts before us a terrific programme, but I am compelled to acknowledge
that there is very little in this statement of
aims which does not carry my enthusiastic
support. To print it may be to lay oneself
open to the charge of publishing " socialist
propaganda ". Yet I can sincerely plead
that I am quite innocent of any political
purpose. If asked the question, " To what
political party do you belong? " I should
have to answer, " To none ". No political
creed as yet outlined seems to be capable of
bringing the Kingdom of Heaven to earth.
The Conservative party is now much more
Liberal than the Liberal party was when
my father gave whole-hearted support to
Gladstone, while the " Socialism " with

which Mr. Ramsay McDonald closed his
career was more conservative than the creed
of many a modern " Tory ".   I have many
Conservative friends and greatly admire
some of the work they do.   On the other
hand, much of the unhappiness of the poor
and the impossibility, under present conditions, of their ever having a fair share
of the good things which God has planned
for *all* His children makes me feel a strong
sympathy with all that Socialism has
laboured to get for the unprivileged.   But
again, so many of my Socialist friends are so
bitter and hostile to all who think differently
from them, their creed has led to such a
soulless materialism in some places where it
has been tried, that I find it quite impossible
to see a new world born from Socialism.
" Socialism ", says D. R. Davies,[1] " one of
the last ramparts of the illusions of modern
men, is no more immune from the curse of
self-destruction than the other expedients
of man to be his own God.   To assume that
men can, by organisation and effort, create
a Christian order in politics implies a fundamentally anti-Christian idea.   It means, in

[1] " The Church and the Peace ", pp. 20 and 29
(Nisbet).

short, that man does not need a redeemer, which indeed is the belief of the modern world. But this is not the position of New Testament Christianity. The New Testament begins with the fact of man's radical corruption. Everything, therefore, which he does is cursed by the contradition of self-destruction. All human achievement, without exception, contains within itself the seed of its own decay be it ever so progressive or humane."

I may be quite wrong, but my own view is that what is wrong is not so much the "ism", but the "ist". Capitalism could be beneficent if the capitalist were a Christian like a friend of mine, who, from being a working lad earning a few shillings a week, is now a millionaire employing many hundreds. He has been kind enough to talk over with me many of his schemes, the profit-sharing scheme, the pension scheme, the five-day-week scheme, all of them now working well at his factory. I know what he has done to ameliorate the conditions under which his people are working, and having talked with the work-people themselves without their knowing that I was a friend of the " boss ", and heard what they

say about him and the well-being provided
by him, I can only wish that all big industrial
concerns went forward in the same spirit.

" Do you find much discontent among the
women and girls? " I asked a forewoman.

" No one leaves here," she said, " except
to get married or go on pension."

" Do you realise how much the boss is
getting compared with you? " I asked a
foreman.

" Yes," he said, " but his brains built up
the business and his brains keep it going,
and I haven't to worry whether it's a good
year or a bad year. I get my wages regular."

My friend the " boss " once asked me if
there was anything in his factory of which
Jesus Christ would disapprove. I could find
nothing. If he sold all and gave to the poor
he would throw hundreds of people out of
work. I cannot see what there is in his
life and work which is wrong.

On the other hand, I know the injustice,
the overbearing tyranny, the conditions
almost of slavery which the capitalist system
makes *possible* to those who misuse power
over their fellows—and how few of us are
fit to have any power over other people's
lives. But would Socialism mean greater

happiness unless worked by socialists of high principles and unselfish ideals? Some experiments tried on a large scale in Europe hardly seem to suggest that either system, *qua* system, will bring into being that happiness, co-operation, increased leisure and culture, that sharing out of life's good things which all right-thinking people wish to see in the age that is to be.

" Changing the Government ", said Studdert Kennedy once, " is no good. It only means taking one set of sinners out and putting another set of sinners in." Perhaps the saying is as profound as it is amusing. We are back, then, at the point made in the first chapter that the supreme need of the world and the only condition in which development can really become progress is the change of heart or conversion of the individual. This simplification of a vast problem is infuriating to many, and of course I do not for one moment mean by " conversion " any adherence to any particular sect or the embracing of any particular creed—a thing which Jesus never seems to have done. I mean a fundamental change of heart and outlook by which man recognises the august majesty of

God as well as His fatherhood, the claim of
God on his life, the dynamic power of God
available in his own life and in the world,
and the secret of inner peace by surrender
to the Divine will.   I mean an attitude to
men which is really brotherly, which sees
there is no " salvation " for anybody, no
hope for the " world ", unless everybody in
the world is included in its scope.   I mean
a humble dependence on God and some
means of communion with Him by which
man has " power to become " in his own life,
and power and *authority* to go out into the
world and translate the love of God into
terms of the traffic of the market place, the
work of the courts, the teaching in the
schools, the selling of goods, the adding up
of figures, the manufacture of articles, the
typing of correspondence, the healing of
bodies and minds, the work of the ministry,
the running of a home, or whatever one's
contribution to the community happens to be.

Jesus, one remembers, did not announce
His Gospel in slogans like " A living wage
for every man." But rather, " Change
your way of looking at life and believe the
good news about God ", which, I claim, is a
fair interpretation of Mark 1[15].

And certainly the Apostles did not go out into a pagan world shouting, " Better homes for heroes." They preached about sin. They said that the first thing to get right in an evil world was the individual's relationship with God. " Be ye reconciled with God." They said that by His death and glorious resurrection, life could be full of beauty, purpose, joy, and meaning, and that life always looked forward in illimitable hope.

I feel quite sure that whatever the duties of others may be, in trying to make a new world after the war, the one job of Christ's Church is to deepen its own religious life by the new dedication of the individual to Christ, and then to spread that glorious infection in the lives of others.

I hope I may be forgiven the personality when I say that the man through whom our present Foreign Secretary, Lord Halifax, became a convinced Christian did a finer piece of work for the Kingdom of God than if he had allowed himself to write to the Prime Minister telling him what our foreign policy ought to be, and the minister of religion, through whom Lord Stamp, one of the greatest economists in the world, became the vital Christian he is, did more for the

Kingdom of Heaven that if, from his pulpit, he had tried to deal with economic problems.

The Church's job is to change the would-be reformer, suggest and encourage the reforms, and condemn unsparingly all in our national and international life that is contrary to the spirit of Christ. It is not the Church's job to work out detail and to suppose that it can speak with authority on technical questions of economics, psychology, sociology, high-finance and international politics.

How infuriating it must be to many able people in our pews to hear either a half-baked " solution " to some of our many national problems, or else to be told with glib complacency that if only statesmen would try the " way of Christ " all our troubles would end at once ! What exactly is " the way of Christ " in regard to unemployment ?

The Church, as such, has not the training, or the mental equipment, or the executive influence to reorganise industry, advise regarding the business of the State or to solve the complex international situations which constantly arise. She would make herself ridiculous and prove herself quite out of her sphere were she thus to interfere.

But if she can show, to those who *have* the equipment, a vision of God and His world as enlightened Christianity sees it, and then send them out to interpret Christ's spirit in those affairs in which they are expert, a new world-order will be ushered in.

It was my privilege recently to be present at a small dinner party attended by members of the Government and other persons of great influence in our country's affairs. I was grateful to God as I realised how many of those around me at the table were sincere and convinced Christians. It would not be fair to mention names, but perhaps I may quote the climax of the whole evening to me, when Mr. Leslie Burgin, who was then Minister of Transport, said that nothing reminded him so much of the prayer meetings so familiar to him in his youth as did the Wednesday morning meetings of the British Cabinet.

To offer men Christ, to get them to accept Him and then interpret their job in His spirit, whatever that job and political " ism " may be, seems to me the supreme task of the Church and her best contribution to the new world.

It may be that our civilisation is dying

and that our generation will see its end.   I
have no faith, no hope left in man without
God.   Civilisation as such has not within it
the seeds of life, let alone progress.   But if
our nation and empire should turn to Him,
even at this the eleventh hour, then Britain
could be, in His hands, an instrument of
good, a harbinger of the Kingdom of Heaven
on earth.   But will the Church see her true
function and act?   Is there enough of the
spirit of Christ in the Church to change the
heart of the world?   I don't know.   The
hour is late.   The enemy is active.   " One
by one the lamps are going out in Europe."
Breathlessly one watches and waits.   Is it
life for Europe or death?   No one knows.
But no one need merely wait.   The first
thing to *do* is to start again at His feet and
to be ready for whatever His will directs;
" to respond to Him without flinching as He
comes in this moment, there to obtain and
accept His strength, undeflected by self-will
and self-love."

O come to my heart, Lord Jesus,
There is room in my heart for Thee.

THE END